PATTERDALE TER

SEAN FRAIN

BULL GHYLL PUBLICATIONS

First published in 2015 by Bull Ghyll Publications
Second Edition 2016

Copyright 2016 Sean Frain

Contact the publisher through Amazon Books

Acknowledgements: I must first of all thank Robin Breay for his candid assistance with producing this book, particularly for shedding light on his mysterious father, Cyril Breay, and many of his excellent terriers. The information Robin provided only confirmed that Cyril Breay was one of the top breeders of working terriers this country has ever produced. This information also confirms that Cyril Breay can rightly be regarded as the founder of Patterdale terriers, though other breeders such as Frank Buck, Jossie Akerigg and Brian Nuttall, also played an important part in the development of this type of working terrier. I must also thank Tony Swift for providing some of the photographs. It is also essential to thank Roger Westmorland who gave me much information regarding Cyril Breay and his terriers when I was researching for my book, *The Lakeland Terrier,* which I have been able to use for this book.

This book is dedicated to Robin Breay, with gratitude

1. ORIGINS

The origins of modern Patterdale terriers are to some extent shrouded in mystery, lost perhaps because of passing years which can now be measured in several decades. But one thing can be stated with certainty and that is that Cyril Breay and Frank Buck played a massive part in the creation of modern strains and that Cyril Breay in particular was the first to breed the powerful headed hard-coated, smooth or slape-coated black and red terriers that have become so popular today.

Legends abound that Cyril Breay came north with his father from South Wales and that they brought with them a strain of working Sealyham terrier which they used primarily for badger digging. However, further research since the publication of my book, *The Patterdale Terrier*, has dispelled this legend as simply a myth. In fact, Breay was born at Middleton, or possibly Killington, during the early 1890s and his father, Wilfred Henry Breay, was the local vicar.

It is true that Cyril Breay did keep a strain of Sealyham terrier until the early 1920s after his interest in fell terriers had been kindled, possibly after having spent some amount of time in the Windermere area where he courted and married a local girl. Breay had associations with the Coniston Foxhounds in those days and I do not doubt that he followed this hunt whenever possible and likely worked his terriers whenever invited to do so by the then Huntsman, George Chapman, who served in this capacity from 1908 to 1932. There is no reason to believe that his father kept terriers, however, as he was a clergyman who held office at Middleton in Westmoreland and there is nothing to indicate that he was in any way interested in working dogs.

From where Breay obtained his strain of working Sealyham terrier is rather a mystery, but, during those early years, otter-hound packs from Wales visited the area in which Breay lived and he may have obtained his terriers from such sources, or possibly someone locally kept Sealyhams which they used for fox and badger digging. Breay once stated that his strain had originated in Wales, but that doesn't necessarily mean that he obtained his first terriers directly from

Wales. He may simply have been referring to Wales because the Sealyham is a Welsh breed. Scottish and Cairn terriers were certainly kept and worked in the Westmorland area, so maybe Sealyham terriers were readily available to Breay who obtained this breed primarily for the digging of badgers and for working fox in the vale where he lived.

How he first developed an interest in working terriers is, again, shrouded in some mystery, but during the early part of the twentieth century the Sedbergh Foxhounds hunted the Lune Valley, so possibly he became a follower until they disbanded when the Great War broke out in 1914. Shortly after this, my research indicates, Breay began his associations with a young lady who lived at Windermere and whenever he could he would follow the Coniston Foxhounds, further developing his interest in more local strains of working terrier.

Not only did Breay hunt with the Coniston Foxhounds at this time, but in 1920 Tommy Robinson set up his pack of Sedbergh and Lunesdale Foxhounds (keeping and working rough and ready fell terriers and quite typey fox terrier types which may have come from the Kendal otter-hounds at Milnthorpe) and from then on Breay had associations with this pack. In fact, it seems he became a regular follower of foxhounds at about this time, for, shortly after, he began breeding terriers which were more suited to working amongst the high fells of Cumberland, Westmorland and North Yorkshire. Sealyham terriers were game, there can be no doubt about that (there are still some working strains being bred today), but they were a little too short in the leg for working the rock earths found on the fells, or for covering rough country found on the fell tops. Breay may also have experienced problems with Sealyhams not being quite up to the cold of the fells, where temperatures are often far lower than those of the vales.

Rough coated Bedlington type terriers were common in Cumberland and Westmorland in those days and the Sedbergh Foxhounds kept such terriers to use with their pack until forced to disband in 1914, so it isn't surprising that Breay would put one of his Sealyham bitches, or possibly a Sealyham/fell cross, to a fell type terrier during the early 1920s. This white bitch was Wendy and she was bred in 1920.

The Coniston Foxhounds on frozen Lake Windermere in 1895

A terrier serving with the Coniston Foxhounds so impressed Breay that he began his strain by using this red dog to mate Wendy. The name of the terrier, or the owner of the terrier, was not provided by Breay when he noted down his breeding programme, but one can safely say that the red dog was probably owned by George Chapman, or maybe his father, Anthony Chapman, who bred terriers which served with the Coniston pack. Breay certainly knew the Chapmans well, as well as the Logan family who were Masters of this hunt, so he would have had no difficulties in using any of their terriers to put onto his bitches. And so began the breeding programme that would give rise to some of the best working terriers ever to go to ground and, ultimately, produce what has become known as the Patterdale terrier.

Cyril Breay continued to follow the Coniston Hunt whenever possible throughout his long lifetime and was asked to use his terriers whenever opportunity arose. One such occasion was in the

Winster Valley, South Lakeland, when hounds had run a fox to ground in a drain. Breay was asked to try his bitch, Tig, and she went like wildfire, bolting the fox quickly, despite its reluctance after being hunted. The late Gary Middleton was in attendance that day and was most impressed with Breay's terrier. Gary returned to this earth shortly after and dug a badger out of the drain with his working Lakeland terrier. Incidentally, the Middleton strain of Lakeland terrier is partly bred out of Cyril Breay's stock, as Gary first began using and breeding terriers from his uncle's farm in Dent. These were fell type terriers and undoubtedly had Breay bloodlines in them from before the mid-1950s, as did most terriers in the north by that time.

A black terrier with Coniston Hunt (c.1920)

2. THE CONISTON RED TERRIER

Of course, without written or spoken evidence from Breay himself, it is impossible to know exactly which Coniston red dog terrier was put to Wendy to begin Breay's famous strain, but it is good to note a few of the dog terriers working with the pack at that time, any one of which could have been used by Breay as a stud for his white bitch.

Crag was one of the Coniston terriers and in November 1922 he went to ground in a big borran earth alongside a bitch named Dot. The fox refused to bolt and was worried below ground. Crag was obviously a game terrier that could both find and finish a fox and is thus a legitimate contender for a terrier that Breay would consider bringing into his own strain (Breay would only use stud dog terriers which were capable of killing a fox).

Crab was another grand terrier serving with the Coniston Foxhounds at that time and he must be the favourite contender for the terrier used by Breay to mate his bitch, Wendy, as Crab became a legend during the 1920s. He was actually owned by Old Anthony Chapman, the father of George Chapman. Crab was a superb terrier and I suspect he may well have been bred from a mix of old Coniston lines, suffused with outcross blood from Tommy Dobson and possibly Joe Bowman. Chapman was great friends with both Dobson and Bowman and likely used their terriers to bring into his own strain.

Once, alongside another terrier named Tiny, Crab succeeded in shifting a fox from a difficult earth in Raven Crag. On another occasion, during the autumn of 1923, Crab was put into the huge rockpiles at Kirkstone Quarry known locally as "rubbish heaps" and stayed almost twenty-four hours to a fox in a difficult spot, alongside another terrier named Nip. The place was far too vast and deep to attempt a dig, but it was thought the pair of terriers had worried their fox below.

In 1924 Crab was in action again, going to ground at Black Crag with Tiny. A fox had been put in by hounds, but another was lurking in the borran at Black Crag. This fresh fox bolted quickly, but the hunted fox stood its ground and was worried in by the game terriers. A large dog fox was dug out after much effort. One of Crab's best efforts was again in 1924 at Brock Crag, where he went to ground on a fox that had been hard-pressed and was thus reluctant to face hounds again. Crab was a game, hard terrier, however, and quickly found his fox in this large rock spot. Crab soon persuaded his foe that the open was probably a safer place and thus it bolted.

*Bruce Logan,
Master of Coniston
Foxhounds*

These were just a few of the many escapades which made Crab a legend in the fells during the 1920s, as he was used extensively for several seasons and proved to be a very game, all-round worker. Breay would undoubtedly have been proud to use Crab, as he was both a finder and killer of foxes. Crab, again working with Tiny, found a fox in a large borran under High Pike on the fells above Ambleside and Rydal, which was duly bolted from this noted stronghold. Again, I cannot conclude that Crab was the red dog from the Coniston Hunt used as a stud dog by Cyril Breay, but I think it very likely, as Breay would use only the best workers on his strain and Crab was probably the very best the Coniston had during the 1920s.

A terrier with the Sedbergh Hunt of a type bred by Cyril Breay during the 1920s/early 1930s

Kelly was another game terrier serving with the Coniston during the 1920s and he was a big, bold Bedlington type who was very game and who would stay with a fox until dug out. Kelly, a terrier walked at Troutbeck Park and one which featured in Clapham's book about hunting in the fells (published in 1920), drew a vixen out of a drain near Raven Crag in 1922 and would undoubtedly have impressed

Breay, who was fascinated by gameness in terriers. Kelly was certainly game. The only problem is that Kelly was wheaten, rather than red, though I have many times witnessed wheaten terriers being referred to as red, so Kelly cannot be ruled out.

On another occasion, in 1924, a fox was run in by hounds at Hallylands in the Troutbeck Valley and Kelly, a terrier walked at Troutbeck Park by a Mrs Leake, was put into the borran. Kelly worried his fox to ground and the brush of the dog fox was presented to Mrs Heelis, otherwise known as Beatrix Potter, the famous children's author. Mrs Heelis was a keen supporter of the Coniston Foxhounds, but was against hunting hares and otters. No doubt, as a sheep farmer, she had experienced losses of lambs to foxes and concluded that they must be hunted if livestock was to be protected to some extent. Kelly worried that fox singlehanded in a place that was not easy to work.

Yet another terrier that could kill a fox which stood its ground was Grip. He served at the Coniston at the same time as Crab and Kelly and once finished a fox below ground near Troutbeck, after bolting it from the same earth earlier in the day. Grip was obviously game and sensible, able to shift a fox and be used to ground again on the very same day.

Pip was another useful sort which served at the Coniston during the 1920s, but he came on the scene about the middle of the decade, which would probably be a little too late to be a contender for the stud used by Breay to mate Wendy. Again, my money would be on Crab being the founding dog terrier of Breay's illustrious strain of what later became known as the Patterdale terrier

3. DESIRED QUALITIES IN A DOG TERRIER

Cyril Breay and, indeed, Frank Buck, had definite views on what they required of a dog terrier and Breay in particular was almost obsessed with the quality of gameness. Gameness is hard to define, but it is a quality that enables a terrier to do its utmost to find and stay with a fox until it bolts, is dug out, or, in the case of several breeds of terrier, is worried underground. Patterdale terriers of the modern era have become famous for their game qualities and many have been first-rate fox killing earth dogs. Breay required his dog terriers to kill any fox that wouldn't bolt and he refused to breed from any that were not capable of worrying an adult dog fox which stood its ground. One thing is certain; that Coniston red dog terrier was not only a very useful worker with hounds, but was also a fox killer, and a singlehanded fox killer at that, otherwise Breay would not have ever considered using it on one of his bitches.

Mrs Spence's Egton Lakelands - part Coniston Foxhounds bred

It is true that many of the terriers working with the fell packs were put to ground in pairs and Crab often worked alongside another terrier, but if Breay used a dog terrier on his bitches then one can be certain that that terrier had proved itself as a singlehanded killer of foxes. Terriers were put to ground in pairs simply because earths in the fells were so vast in area that it often took more than one terrier to pin a fox down, as these could move around larger borrans avoiding a single terrier for hours at a time. Once pinned down, there was usually only enough room for one terrier to work the fox and the gamest did most of the work, as the gamest was the most determined to be at its fox. Gameness and the ability to finish a fox were of utmost importance to Breay, but he did not seem to put as much importance on coat type as others who hunted the fell country. Breay kept terriers with varying coat types ranging from scruffy Bedlington type jackets to smooth, or slape coats. Others had the tight, wiry coat similar to that of the Irish, Border and original Patterdale terriers. Cyril Breay, although starting with short-legged Sealyham terriers, much preferred his stock to be leggy and he found success with terriers as tall as fifteen or even sixteen inches at the shoulder, as long as they were spannable (having a narrow chest that would allow them to negotiate the tricky limestone earths found in the areas he mostly hunted). He also preferred a terrier to have a good strong head and jaw, though some of his terriers, especially some of those he bred pre-1940s, were rather weaker in the heads than much of his later stock.

Cyril Breay favoured black terriers during the 1950s. Patterdale terriers belonging to Paul Stead

Colour didn't seem to be an issue with Breay, though he did like a black terrier, especially when this colouring became dominant during the 1950s. Breay's terriers ranged from brown to blue and tan, black and tan, red, wheaten and black, with some pied colouring also appearing in litters. But it was that quality of gameness that superseded all others and Breay always put the gamest dog terriers to the gamest bitch terriers, thus producing the gamest offspring.

4. ORIGINS OF BLACK PATTERDALES

Cyril Breay's Gem, as far as my research indicates, was the first of the black bull terrier type Patterdales to appear in Breay and Buck's strain, but the black colouring itself was already appearing in litters long before the 1950s.

Willie Irving, writing to working Bedlington terrier and working registered Lakeland terrier enthusiast George Newcombe during the 1960s, stated that black terriers were common in the Windermere and Grasmere districts and that Breay and Buck's black strain had originated from those areas. And Irving, as it turned out, was correct in his carefully thought-out assumptions.

Ernie Towers and Jim Fleming were the top breeders in Grasmere during the early to mid-part of the twentieth century and these undoubtedly produced black terriers in their respective strains. Brait' Black was another famous follower of the Coniston Foxhounds at that time and he too bred some black terriers in his strain, as did George and Anthony Chapman, the father of George and owner of Crab. This Coniston blood, as we have seen, was used to found Breay's strain and so black terriers were no doubt appearing in litters bred by him as far back as the 1920s, though photographic proof that black terriers were not unkown among Breay's stock before the 1950s only exists from the late 1930s, as far as I know.

The Coniston terriers also influenced Irving's strain of working registered Lakeland terriers and he too bred occasional black terriers, one of the most important of which was a bitch named Myrt which was sold as a puppy to Jim Fleming of Grasmere in 1937 or 1938. Irving actually delivered Myrt when she was a puppy, travelling over to Grasmere to Jim Fleming's farm once she was old enough to leave her dam. Myrt was a near-black terrier, rather than a true black, but still, she obviously carried genes which produced this colouring (Irving's strain was a mix of Eskdale and Ennerdale, Coniston, Blencathra (through Blencathra Turk), Douglas paisley, Mrs Spence's Egton terriers, Oregill Lakelands and Jack and Frank Pepper strain Lakelands (from the Bowderstone prefix), as well as others from various backgrounds.

Mrs *Spence's home at Howtown where the Egton strain of Lakeland terrier was bred, which had some influence on Breay/Buck breeding. Ullswater can be seen in the background*

Myrt served at the Ullswater Foxhounds during the war years, being loaned by Fleming from 1939 onwards, but it was Willie Irving who bred her, despite the fact that this bitch terrier is commonly known as Jim Fleming's Myrt. Brian Plummer, writing in his book *The Fell Terrier*, stated that Myrt was the Magna Mater of all modern strains and so her contribution to working terrier bloodlines was tremendous, to say the least. Her sire was Tinker, a son of the famous Turk of Melbreak, and her dam was Tess, a daughter of Gypsy of Melbreak and Deepdale Holloa, otherwise known as Rock, the leggy terrier in Irving's famous Crummock Water photograph taken in 1936. It is probably Gypsy of Melbreak who is coupled to Rock at Irving's feet.

Gypsy became a legend during the late 1930s and early 1940s and enjoyed almost celebrity status throughout the western regions of the Lake District, where Irving's terriers were eagerly sought. To illustrate the hardiness of Irving's strain of pedigree Lakeland terrier we can do no better than consult newspaper articles written during the 1930s which reported on a tragedy involving Gypsy of Melbreak.

Willie Irving with (L-R) Peggy, Gypsy of Melbreak? & Rock (Deepdale Holloa)

The Melbreak Foxhounds met at the Fish Inn, Buttermere, on November 28th 1941 and a fox was roused from Knott Rigg, with a fast hunt developing. Reynard took hounds through Keskadale Yaks and down into the lovely Newlands Valley. The hunt took in a vast area of this majestic vale, but hounds pushed their fox hard as it made towards the head of the valley, climbing Robinson Fell and going to ground at an awkward spot at Robinson Crag.

Now in her fifth season, Gypsy of Melbreak was put to ground after Willie had arrived soon after hounds began marking and she found and bolted her quarry, which made out across a very narrow ledge amongst the sheer-drop crags. Gypsy soon emerged in pursuit of her fox and followed its course across the huge jutting crags, but she lost her footing and fell down the crag face for some considerable distance, with a sickening bump or two along the way. The poor terrier was badly injured and had to be carried back to kennels, but she went on to make a full recovery and saw yet more work with hounds. This incident was widely reported by the Cumbrian newspapers and references made to Gypsy betrayed the fact that by 1941 she had become a very well known terrier in the area.

Jim Fleming's Myrt, a granddaughter of Gypsy of Melbreak, was mated to Ullswater Rock, a leggy black and tan son of Egton Rock of Howtown, Mrs Graham Spence's famous terrier and a show champion. Ullswater Rock was loaned to Anthony Barker who hunted the Ullswater Foxhounds during the war years (1939-1945) by Joe Wilkinson, the brother of Sid Wilkinson who was probably the top breeder of working Lakelands in the Ullswater country from the 1930s until the 1970s. Ullswater Rock was a hard terrier that was used to finish lamb or poultry killing foxes. From this union came Tear 'Em, Judy and Jim. Tear 'Em was a near-black terrier, but Jim was true black and this terrier was used during the post-war years by Willie Irving at the Melbreak.

Judy was kept and used by Anthony Barker, becoming an ancestress of Barker's incredibly game dog terrier, Rock, the sire of Sid Wilkinson's Rock; possibly the most influential stud in working Lakeland terrier history and another grand worker, whilst Tear 'Em, owned by Jim Fleming, was loaned to Joe Wear who took up his post as Huntsman of the Ullswater again after returning from the war. Tear 'Em became a famous fox killer and he once slew three foxes in one day's hunting, so Breay and Buck brought bitches to

Tear 'Em and yet more black colouring went into the mix. It was a son of Tear 'Em who mated Breay's Gem and bred Buck's Black Davy; a terrier which was one-quarter Scottish terrier bred. Skiffle was probably a litter sister to Davy. Skiffle and Davy then went on to have a massive influence on future breeding and one can safely say that all modern strains of Patterdale terrier, as well as many strains of working fell terrier, including my own, are descended from this pair of elegant and game terriers.

The Ullswater terriers had quite an influence on Breay and Buck's breeding policies and there is photographic proof that quite typey black Lakeland terriers were serving at the Ullswater during the 1940s which may well have been bred out of Jim Fleming's Myrt. It is possible that such black terriers also mated Breay and Buck bitches, though this can only be educated guesswork. Breay only provided a very basic pedigree of his dogs, but far more terriers were used in the mix, such as dogs from Jossie Akerigg, Joe Dobbinson, the one-time terrierman for the Zetland Foxhounds, and Harry Hardisty at the Melbreak.

Photographic proof that black terriers served at the Ullswater Hunt during the late 1940s. Joe Weir with his son and daughter

Through Black Davy, Scottish terrier blood played a part in bringing about not only the black colouring for which Breay and Buck's terriers became famous, but also the powerful, large heads which became common from the 1950s onwards. And, I do not doubt, the black colouring partly came about from the influence of bull terrier blood, but whether or not Breay and Buck deliberately used a dog or bitch bred out of bull terrier stock remains an unanswered question. One thing is for certain though, that from whatever source it came, bull terrier blood was part of the Breay/Buck strain, as all terriers have at least some bull blood in their breeding.

Small black pit bull terriers were not uncommon in the north during the nineteenth and early twentieth centuries and so it is reasonable to assume that terriers descended from such dogs had some sort of influence on Patterdale strains. Their type betrays this fact. What can be said for a certainty is that black terriers did not originate with Breay and Buck's breeding policies, this colour appearing in litters long before Breay took up with working terriers (records prove that black terriers existed in Norfolk and were used with hunts as early as the eighteenth century, so perhaps black terriers were not uncommon throughout the country during future centuries). Neither did black terriers begin appearing in litters bred by Breay and Buck during the 1950s, as is commonly stated, for black terriers were appearing in litters long before this decade.

Black terriers have existed for centuries

5. ORIGINS OF THE PATTERDALE TERRIER NAME

It is worth noting that Cyril Breay, Frank Buck and breeders associated with them, such as Jossie Akerigg, did not refer to this type of terrier as a Patterdale. Breay just called them black fell terriers, fell terriers or working terriers, nothing more, but the name of Patterdale terrier has stuck and seems to have been used from the 1960s onwards. But from where did this name originate?

Some may be disappointed to discover that Patterdale Village is hardly connected to the modern Patterdale terrier and my research leads me to conclude that this name first began being used with regard to this type of working terrier in the Rossenendale Valley and South Pennine areas of East Lancashire and West and South Yorkshire. It seems that this name was already being used during the 1960s when Breay was still doing the rounds at various shows, where he enjoyed considerable success I might add, but it was during the 1970s that this name really began to stick and become popular.

Brian Plummer was furious about the use of this name and made his thoughts on the subject clear for all to read in *The Fell Terrier* and in articles he wrote for *Shooting Times*, but even his protestations at the time could do nothing to alter the fact that Breay and Buck's type of terrier would from then on be known as Patterdale terriers. Breay and Buck's dogs had a massive influence in the areas just mentioned where the name of Patterdale terrier first began to be used, as the terrier lads hunting the moors and mountains of the Pennine Chain found this strain to be ideal for working most of the earths to be found in these districts, which range from stone drains to rock-piles found mostly in old quarry workings, some of which are incredibly deep.. One of the deepest is to be found at the top of an old quarry on Holcombe Moor near Ramsbottom and only the best of terriers could work this place. A terrier lad I know has bred Breay/Buck stock for decades and he has bolted foxes from this spot with his terriers on numerous occasions. Tim Poxton's bitch, Mocky, a daughter of Arthur Nixon's first class worker, Sam, once bolted a fox from this earth which had been run in by the Holcombe Harriers.

Someone once said that Breay's terriers were good workers if the earths were not too deep, but that is nonsense. Breay's terriers were at their very best in deep earths and the fact that so many used Breay and Buck's strain in the difficult Pennine areas where vastly deep earths abound is testimony enough to this fact. It can also be said with certainty that most of the earths Breay worked with his terriers were deep, dangerous places, so a terrier strain that couldn't work well in deep earths would have been of no use to him. Disregard claims that Breay/Buck terriers were weak in deep earths, as nothing could be further from the truth.

Roger Westmorland's Squeak in winning ways – a looker & first class worker of a type bred by Breay & Buck during the 1950s/60s

Nigel Hinchliffe of the Pennine Foxhounds told Brian Plummer of the abilities of Breay/Buck stock when he was challenged by someone who believed he had better terriers. Hinchliffe allowed the challenger first go after a fox was run into a difficult rock earth in an old quarry, but the leggy Lakeland couldn't get into the actual earth because of large rocks surrounding it. Hinchliffe's terrier was then given a chance and it slid down the slab of rock situated close to the entrance, disappeared below ground, found and bolted the fox and then promptly returned to Hinchliffe.

Breay and Buck's terriers, although finding use in a wide variety of earths, were used predominantly in rock and so the abilities of this strain make them ideal for Pennine areas. Having said this, it is true that Buck used his terriers in lowland areas much of the time where dug-out rabbit holes and drains make up most of the fox dens, as he was terrierman for at least two North Yorkshire packs, but he also hunted the fells of the Yorkshire Dales, predominantly Wensleydale, Coverdale and Swaledale, where rock earths abound.

The Pennines are littered with old quarries and they now make ideal places for foxes to escape the elements. Rarely are foxes not found skulking in these rock-piles when the weather turns nasty and many a fox have I bolted or dug out of such dens, though I must admit that I have had to leave quite a few to ground too, after they have got into a tight spot where the terriers couldn't quite get and where I could not hope to dig. I freely admit to having been bested a time or two by foxes, especially when working rock-piles, but I take comfort in knowing that both Breay and Buck suffered similar disappointments at times.

Robin Breay told me of frustrating times for his father, Cyril, when he would attempt to catch foxes which were proving rather evasive. Above Leck Fell House, high on Leck Fell itself, are to be found a long line of rock-piles which over the years have housed vast numbers of rabbits, even in these post-myxomatosis days. In the spring vixens will dig into these rabbit holes which often lead into the rocks and Breay would go there with the local gamekeeper who was intent on protecting his game-birds, as Leck Fell was once a very important grouse shoot. Breay carried out much fox control in this area, but he found this place difficult.

He would often find evidence of vixen and cubs lurking somewhere amongst the stone-piles, which are commonly known as Leck Fell Stone-beds, but his terriers, although managing to account for a cub or two, would become frustrated after hours on end of attempting to reach their quarry, their master even more frustrated as he dug in only to discover that he too could not get to where vixen and cubs were hiding. Having said this, there were times when Breay succeeded in digging out foxes from this place and on one occasion he and the Leck gamekeeper Arthur Swettenham, dug out a well grown litter on February 23rd during the war years, which is early for a litter of fell foxes in particular, or any litter of foxes come to that!

The difficulties of getting foxes from near-impossible earths meant that those attempting to control predator numbers had to be resourceful. One snowy day in 1960 Robin Breay and Arthur Swettenham entered a terrier into a large rabbit hole known as 'The City' after Arthur had tracked a fox to this den. The terrier stayed all day, but couldn't quite reach its fox and the earth was just too deep to attempt a dig, though they didn't want to give this fox best, so undoubtedly it had killed livestock and had to be accounted for. Robin and the keeper blocked the fox in, but when they returned the next day the fox had managed to dig itself out of the earth.

That day, two fields further up the fell, Robin found a fox lurking in a deep sandy hole and the terrier stayed below, but again this proved a difficult place and so Robin fetched his father late in the day. However, even Cyril Breay and his terriers could not get the fox out of this earth, so Arthur Swettenham set a trap in the hole and succeeded in accounting for it. It is thought that the fox found in that deep sandy hole was the one they had attempted to get out of 'The City' on the previous day. This was a frustrating episode for the terriers especially, but also for the keeper and terrier enthusiasts involved.

On another occasion, when Robin Breay was staying with Frank Buck and his family for a week's holiday, Robin accompanied Buck as he tried a few earths with his terriers, again in the springtime. Buck took his terriers to yet another rock earth on Addleborough, the famous flat-topped fell in Wensleydale which often featured in the BBC TV series *All Creatures Great and Small*, where they keenly marked. A vixen with cubs lurked somewhere among the rocks, but this proved another bad place and in the end, frustrated after hours of trying to get at their foxes, Buck and Robin finally gave them best and left them for another day, Frank's terriers not able to quite get into those tight spaces. In a soil earth a terrier can often dig on, but in rock the walls of the den are unyielding and so if a terrier cannot get to its fox, then one has no chance of accounting for it. On a number of occasions both Breay and Buck were forced to leave foxes to ground, which proves they were mere mortals after all!!!

A place already mentioned where Breay sometimes had frustratingly fruitless digs was at "The City" which was a vast rabbit warren centuries old, situated on the south face of Casterton Low Fell (this fell adjoins Barbon Low Fell). The gamekeeper, Arthur Swettenham, tracked yet another fox in the snow and prints clearly led into the "City." The keeper called Breay out and he soon arrived with his terriers, accompanied by his son, Robin. The terriers, as always, were extremely keen and Breay tried one after the other, but again, they just couldn't get to their foxes, which was a vixen with cubs. After yet more wasted hours, the vixen and her offspring were left in and it was an unhappy journey home for Breay, who was used to enjoying great success with his terriers. But even the very best working terriers cannot account for every fox they are entered to.

6. AN UNLIKELY LIFELONG FRIENDSHIP

Cyril Breay and Frank Buck could not have been more different if they had tried. Breay was a very private man who stayed clear of any sort of attention and he was rather secretive about his breeding programme, confiding mostly in Frank Buck, though he did give a written pedigree to Wally Wild of the Grove and Rufford Hunt in Nottinghamshire during the latter days of his life, when terrier breeding and terrier work were becoming too much for him. The 1960s saw the decline of Breay, who, until that time, was an incredible fell walker, and that is no exaggeration.

Robin tells tales of his father walking home from a day's hunting and having to cover distances of up to twenty miles, after Breay had already spent the day walking miles on the fells following hounds or tracking foxes in the snow. And once, Breay walked home to High Casterton from Ingleton after he had spent the day hunting that district with the Batty's; a family of sporting farmers who kept some excellent terriers and who frequently hunted with Breay at Kingsdale and other locations close to the huge bulk of Ingleborough Fell. In fact, Breay often hunted Ingleborough itself and he took many foxes from a rock earth near the top of the fell known locally as 'The Arks.' This was not an easy place for Breay's terriers to work, yet he bolted and shot several from this noted stronghold.

Cyril Breay's home at High Casterton

Breay had two children with his first wife and two with his second wife, but he found it difficult to show affection, being a very private man. One day his daughter from his first marriage, after asking her father again and again to fund a course at Agricultural College for cheese-making and after having been repeatedly rebuffed for her troubles, decided to sell the family's chicken coup and all the chickens in order to obtain the money she needed. When Breay returned home to Mallerstang he discovered his beloved chickens were gone and never spoke to his daughter for years afterwards. He seemed to have depressive episodes too, especially after losing a terrier to ground or after having one killed by badgers, when he would talk to none of his family, or at the very least grunt at them.

Frank Buck, on the other hand, was a very friendly, outgoing sort of person who was the life and soul of any party, and he particularly enjoyed the "sport" of "tourist baiting." Exactly who first began "tourist baiting" is difficult to say, but my money would be on 'Auld' Will Ritson of Wasdale Head in the Western Lake District. Coincidentally, Breay and Buck's strain of terrier may well have been descended from that of Ritson's, as he was one of the top breeders of the original Patterdale terrier during the nineteenth century.

Will Ritson of Wasdale Head

Will Ritson was born at Row Foot Farm, Wasdale Head, in 1808 and he was, like John Peel, a sporting statesman farmer who hunted the Scawfell Foxhounds and was instrumental in setting up the Ennerdale Foxhounds, which were later bought by Willie Porter to form the Eskdale and Ennerdale Foxhounds, though Tommy Dobson, the former of the Eskdale Hunt, had the Ennerdale Foxhounds on loan for several years before Porter finally purchased them after Dobson's death in 1910.

Although the tourist industry had taken off during the 1700s, it wasn't until the mid-1800s that Wasdale became a popular place for visitors who were intent on enjoying the challenging fells and crags of this wild and bleak district. Ritson, having a good business head on his shoulders, decided to turn part of his farm into an inn and he applied for a licence to sell alcohol, which was duly granted. He named his new business the Huntsman's Inn and the food, drink and accommodation he provided soon attracted visitors to the area, whom he "baited" with tall stories. Some believed him, others were sceptical, while some thought him rather an eccentric fool, but most liked him and the inn was packed to the rafters during dark evenings when the fells and crags could not be scaled.

There were many wild nights at the inn and Ritson would regale visitors with his stories, one being of 'flying foxes' he had bred by crossing local eagles with foxes to produce a race of creatures he hunted with his hounds, but could never catch as they would take to their wings whenever hounds got a little too close. He also told them about the turnips he had grown as winter fodder for his sheep, which were so huge his cattle disappeared from view after eating their way into them. Will was known as a "reet good fibber" and his stories inspired the 'World's Biggest Liar' competition which is still held today at Santon Bridge. Ritson, it is said, actually won the competition when he stated, "I cannot tell a lie."

Another tall tale of his may well have turned into a local legend still told today, of the disappearing corpse of a local woman. A young man had tragically died in the Wasdale region and a horse was pulling a cart on which his coffin was laid along what are known in the Lakes as Corpse Roads; routes over the fells from isolated villages to churchyards where burials took place. This Corpse Road was one of the loneliest of them all, leading from Wasdale Head across bleak, windswept Burnmoor to Eskdale. Something, it is said, spooked the horse and off it went, running onto the high fells and disappearing in a murky, black, swirling mist which clung to the high places that day. Although a search party was organised and all the local area was well covered by folk who knew the ground intimately, no sign of the coffin was found.

A short time later his mother, no doubt deeply distressed at what had occurred to her son's body and being unable to bury him, also passed away and yet another funeral was organised, another tramp along that long and lonely Corpse Road being necessary. During her funeral, however, that horse was also spooked by something and it too ran off and disappeared. Yet another search was organised, but this time the local folk were more successful in their endeavours and a coffin was found. Amazingly, the coffin was the one her son was to be buried in and the body of his mother, according to this legend, was never found. That has to be one of Will Ritson's tall tales, hasn't it?!!!

No doubt quite a number of Lake District folk tales have their origins in the snug of the Huntsman's Inn where Ritson's stories became legendary and the legend of the Wild Dog of Ennerdale may also have either originated with Will Ritson, or he embellished it, as he told visitors to the inn fascinating tales of his father's exploits during this hunt in the early part of the nineteenth century.

According to legend, the first indications that some terrible and mysterious beast was on the loose was in the early spring of 1810 when farmers in the west of Cumbria began to find some of their sheep had been savaged by some sort of wild animal. The beast would kill and feed on an average of a half-dozen or so sheep each time during the first few nights and so the farmers of the area, including Ritson's father, held a meeting and unanimously decided that something must be done to put a stop to these unforgivable crimes; the intolerable savaging among their livestock which, after all, was badly affecting their livelihoods. In fact, had the killings continued for any length of time it was likely the farmers would finally have become bankrupt. At first nobody knew what was killing the sheep, but a dog was the main suspect. Farm collies can sometimes turn to sheep killing, but all the farm dogs in the area could be accounted for, and, anyway, the injuries to the sheep were not consistent with a simple case of sheep-worrying, nor were the large numbers of sheep falling victim to the wild beast that was preying on them so effectively. One evening, however, a shepherd from either Ennerdale or Wasdale chanced upon the beast as it fed on a dying sheep and he described it as some sort of dog, perhaps an unusually large type of lurcher, which had obviously turned wild, as it fled the scene as soon as it saw his approach.

From that night on things became even more frustrating for the local shepherds as the dog seemed to possess a similar cunning to that of a fox. The animal was unlike any dog known to local folk and much speculation spread throughout the district. In those days gypsies often travelled around the Lakeland farms buying poor grade wool which they would sell on at markets, and it was these who were blamed for turning the dog loose. However, if this legend is indeed true, I believe the dog may have escaped from some sort of travelling circus. If descriptions supposedly given at the time are to be believed then this dog may well have been a mastiff/wolf hybrid, or possibly some sort of mutant mastiff resulting from very close inbreeding, being part of a circus "freak" show.

It is difficult to say, but one thing is certain and that is that this dog was not of any known and recognised breed. It is also possible that it was some sort of wild dog captured in Africa and paraded around with a circus until it finally escaped and was forced to survive by feeding off sheep which were readily found out on the fells of Cumberland.

The beast was cunning in that it often struck different flocks each night, never attacking the same flock two nights running, and mostly preyed upon sheep during the hours of darkness when shepherds found it almost impossible to guard their flocks to any great effect. Its territory ranged for several miles in the West Cumbrian fell districts and several different flocks were affected.

In the end the shepherds banded together and formed a pack of hounds, terriers, collies and street curs with which they hunted down the wild beast that had so plagued their flocks. The wild dog showed yet more cunning when it was found by the hunters to be sheltering in places among the rocks and crags from where it could see anyone approaching from quite a distance away. What makes me think that this wild dog may have been of African origin, or a wolf hybrid, is that the hounds and other dogs took to hunting it readily, which would have been very unlikely had this been some sort of domestic breed. The hunts became legendary, as the wild dog was able to keep ahead of hounds and hunters and often gave long runs in the West Cumberland area; sometimes heading for the coast before turning inland again and heading back to the high fells.

According to legend, these hunts were talked about for decades afterwards and so, if based on truth, some exaggeration must be allowed for. For instance, it was reported many decades later that as many as three hundred sheep were killed by the beast, but could it have been more like thirty in reality? It is impossible to say, but stories tell of a wild dog running loose for quite some time in and around Ennerdale and Wasdale and that it caused quite a lot of damage to the shepherds' livelihoods. Legend has it that the wild dog would sometimes wait for the leading hound to approach and then it would attack and drive it off, leaving it with quite severe injuries, before fleeing from the rest of the pack. However, I think it more likely that the beast hid among rocks and crag ledges and that terriers getting more easily into such places were often the ones to be savaged by the wild dog, though some hounds were also injured. The shepherds tried all sorts of methods to catch the culprit, including poisoning carcasses it was feeding upon and carrying guns at night in an attempt to get in a lucky shot, but nothing worked and so the long and arduous hunts continued. Legend also states that one of the local shepherds saw the dog from only a few yards distance, but his gun misfired and as a consequence the beast fled unharmed.

By mid-summer of 1810 quite a large bounty was offered for the capture of the wild dog and so this attracted hunters from all across the Lakes. John Peel was one of the keenest of all hunters in the Lakes at the time and he may well have joined in this determined effort to capture the sheep-worrying beast, as Peel was certainly one of those who hunted predators and claimed the bounties offered on carcasses by church wardens acting for landowners. Peel often covered some of the areas where the wild beast was hunted, so it seems reasonable to assume he may well have been involved.

Another who very likely joined in the chase if these stories are indeed true was the Master of the Melbreak Foxhounds, Mr William Pearson of Bannock, which he had formed in 1807, only three years before these incidents are supposed to have occurred. In fact, many of the districts where these hunts were enacted, were areas hunted by the Melbreak Foxhounds in those dim and distant days, though there were also many other packs mostly kept by farmers for the hunting-down of any predator which attacked their flocks.

One summer morning hounds roused the wild dog and it led them all the way to Wasdale, on the fells above the valley where Ritson's father farmed. The beast then headed into the low country and hounds hunted it all the way to the coastal district surrounding Drigg Village, but hounds had to be stopped here as it was nearly dark. Another legendary hunt saw the beast heading along the outskirts of Ennerdale, past Lamplugh and Dean Village, on through the mining district of Clifton until being lost not far from Cockermouth, close to the river. Another hunt began when the wild dog was spotted in the Ennerdale area and it actually ran through Ennerdale Bridge. It is said that a large crowd followed hounds until their quarry was once again lost near Cockermouth. Yet another hunt saw hounds hunting from Ennerdale, through Egremont and all the way to St Bees after traversing the big pastures in this district, as well as woodlands scattered about the area, with a wild storm eventually washing away all traces of scent. This storm saved the beast from almost certain capture, as this was a particularly good and fast hunt. The beast was disturbed in a field once again a few days later and took hounds back to St Bees, but once more it escaped. All efforts were proving fruitless and yet more sheep were savaged and partly-eaten by the wild dog, so the shepherds grew more and more frustrated.

By the back-end of summer the local farmers were frustrated beyond belief, but they were also more determined than ever to catch the sheep-killer. Whilst harvesting, a farmer spotted the beast lurking in a field of ripe corn. Men and hounds were gathered and the beast, on being flushed, was wounded by gunshot, but got away. Hounds went away in pursuit, however, with the odds now stacked a little more in their favour. A long hunt ensued in the River Ehen district and one of the farmers eventually caught up with the beast in a wood near to the river, where he at last shot it dead, the hounds having brought it to bay.

Legends state that the wild beast had preyed on sheep for several months and had possibly killed many more than thirty in that time, though three hundred does seem a little excessive, but certainly not impossible. It is said that the carcass of the beast was carried in triumph all the way back to one of the Ennerdale Bridge alehouses, where celebrations went on well into the night. The beast was skinned and its hide was reputedly displayed for many years in a museum at Keswick. This was likely Hutton's Museum. Ritson's father may well have passed on a true account to his son, but one can imagine Will Ritson embellishing the facts until little of the truth was left, the early rock climbers engrossed in his tales as they supped ale and spirits back at the Huntsman's Inn.

Frank Buck may not have been in the same league as Ritson when it came to "tourist baiting" but he was certainly a good storyteller and he enjoyed 'winding' people up with tall tales. Young folk flocked to both Breay and Buck and Frank, before selling them a puppy, or parting with sound advice regarding the working of terriers, would regale them with his stories, though, obviously, some of the stories were true, such as the one about his favourite terrier, Tex, taking over 100 foxes in just one season from the Pennhill area of Wensleydale.

Like Breay, Buck would track foxes in the snow, a method used for well over a century at that time by local gamekeepers intent on raising large numbers of game-birds for shooting, rather than for providing food for wild predators, and then bolt them with his terriers, shooting them as they fled from the earth. Buck, like Breay, was a great shot and over the years he took hundreds of foxes using this method. When snow wasn't on the ground, Buck would visit large numbers of earths with his terriers and rely on them to tell him whether or not they were inhabited, which meant his dogs had to posses good noses or they were as good as useless. Most days Buck found foxes to ground, but he also had a few blank days, like the rest of us.

Walter Parkin with a terrier rescued from a bad Place at Leck Fell

Frank Buck was born at Appersett on the outskirts of Hawes and he was keen on ferreting when a lad and a young man, but he took seriously to terrier work after meeting Cyril Breay who gave him his first terrier of note. This was during the 1930s and by that time

Breay had already established a seriously good and capable strain of working terrier which were proving themselves useful in some of the deepest earths in Britain – earths which were also incredibly dangerous and which, across the decades, claimed the lives of a small number of his terriers, as Breay was very careful about where he put his terriers and rarely were his dogs lost, though several were trapped over the years. One of these was Barker.

Barker was bred out of an East Kent Hunt terrier and Breay's bitch, Whiskers, which was red in colour and was bred out of Tubby, one of the offspring resulting from the Wendy/Coniston red dog mating. Barker became an exceptionally good working bitch and she not only bolted foxes to guns, but she also saw service with the Lunesdale Foxhounds after their formation in 1930 when Tommy Robinson ran on a few hounds until the Lunesdale Foxhounds became firmly established in 1936.

One day whilst Breay was following the Lunesdale pack (my research indicates the year to have been 1936, when Walter Parkin first began whipping-in to Tommy Robinson, becoming the Huntsman of the Lunesdale Foxhounds in 1948, though he hunted hounds on many occasions for Robinson before his official appointment as Huntsman), a fox was run into a difficult rock spot at Bishopdale; a wild, remote dale which is visited by very few tourists, even today, and Breay was asked to try Barker, alongside one of his other bitches. This bitch had been given this name because of a peculiar trait she displayed whilst at work. Breay often ran her loose and if she found an occupied earth or warren, she would bark until Breay arrived, which didn't always suit him. When ferreting or working fox earths, Breay did his utmost to go about his business in complete silence, hoping that the rabbits, or foxes, would bolt quickly and without any hesitation, so Barker must have irritated Breay whenever she kicked up a fuss in this manner.

Barker and the other bitch entered this large rock earth and soon found their fox skulking below ground, which they worried, but in the process of tackling their fox they became trapped among the rocks, perhaps the corpse of the fox blocking their exit. A pound for every terrier trapped by the corpse of a fox it has just worried would yield quite a considerable sum if ever records were kept. A hard, gruelling dig ensued and Barker was reached first and she was got out safely, but the other bitch was in a far more difficult spot and after a few days Breay began to think that a rescue was now impossible. It was then that Walter Parkin, the famous Huntsman of the Lunesdale Foxhounds who was at that time acting as Whipper-in to Tommy Robinson, informed Breay that he knew of a chap whom he thought could help.

Frank Buck after a successful rescue in the 1950s

Breay agreed to Walter calling in his friend, but he still felt that further attempts to reach the trapped bitch were hopeless. However, the outgoing and cheerful Frank Buck arrived and his disposition and positive outlook gave Breay some hope. Breay went into deep depressions whenever his terriers were in seemingly hopeless situations and he would barely talk to anyone around him, but Buck's cheerful, positive nature made quite an impression on Breay and digging operations resumed with gusto, in spite of the fact that the weather had by that time turned very nasty indeed as snow blizzards and icy conditions swept across the dale.

Progress was slow and even Frank Buck, chilled to the bone, struggled to keep optimistic, yet he, along with a few quarrymen he knew and whom he had brought along with him, set explosives and blasted the nigh-on unyielding rock until, at last, the other trapped bitch was reached and pulled out of what would have become her grave, if it hadn't been for Buck's efforts and expertise, along with that of the quarrymen from whom Buck had learnt how to blast safely through rock when rescuing terriers. Buck rescued many terriers during his lifetime and I have in my possession copies of letters sent to Frank after he had successfully rescued trapped terriers; one from a rock den in Coverdale which was trapped for five days in March 1956, and another from yet another bad place above Hawes, though I cannot decipher the exact year this rescue took place. He also rescued Tex and Chew from a crag earth at Addleborough during the 1950s,

Breay's bitch had been trapped for several days, yet she was in rather good shape when pulled from that prison and she had worked deep into that earth. She was a tough bitch and Buck was impressed. Breay was impressed too and was so grateful to Frank Buck that he offered him money for working so hard to rescue his terrier. Buck refused the money offered by Breay, asking for a puppy out of the bitch his efforts had helped to free from that nightmare earth, but Breay went one better. He gave Frank the bitch he had rescued and she was Tiger, one of Buck's best ever terriers and a cornerstone of the Breay and Buck breeding programme, which had its roots in that long and extremely gruelling Bishopdale terrier rescue.

Tiger, given to Frank Buck by Cyril Breay

In fact, that rescue cemented a lifelong friendship between Cyril Breay and Frank Buck and Breay was extremely fond of Buck, more especially for his efforts to get Tiger out of that rock hole. Buck worked tirelessly and, what is more, refused money as a reward. From then on he had a special place in Breay's affections, in spite of this being one of the most unlikeliest of friendships.

Cyril Breay had his kennels along this wall at his High Casterton home

*A chocolate Patterdale terrier similar
to some of Breay's during the 1950s & 1960s*

7. THE BEDLINGTON INFLUENCE

Claims that Cyril Breay simply carried on the breeding programme of Tommy Dobson can now be dismissed as inaccurate, but that doesn't mean that Bedlington terrier blood was not used in the creation and development of modern Patterdale terriers. During the early 1920s the red dog serving with the Coniston Foxhounds was unquestionably of the old Coniston bloodlines and these, together with most terriers in the Lakes at that time, were heavily soused with Bedlington terrier blood. Even the old type of Patterdale terrier had some Bedlington terrier influence and this was obvious by its coat type. True, this strain of terrier was famed for its tight, harsh, weatherproof coat, but only after being stripped out. When left to grow, even the old type of Patterdale would finish up with a long, scruffy jacket which was not as efficient at keeping the weather ay bay as it might have been.

During the nineteenth century and even during the decades preceding the Second World War Cumberland was famed for its game and good quality Bedlington terriers and they were popular and numerous in the districts around Keswick in particular, especially during the middle period of the 1800s when Tommy Dobson was working as a bobbin turner in the Keswick area.

Tommy Dobson with a Bedlington influenced fell terrier

Legends state that Tommy Dobson brought Bedlington terrier blood into his strain during the 1880s when taking his bitches to stud dogs owned by the Kitchen family at Egremont. But Dobson surely brought such blood into his strain long before then and I believe he may well have first used Bedlington terrier blood during his time at Keswick in the mid-1800s. Certainly, Dobson used Bedlington outcross blood again during the 1880s, but it is questionable whether or not he went to the Kitchens at Egremont to obtain such game bloodlines, as is popularly believed. In fact, such game blood was available to Tommy just up the road from Eskdale at Ennerdale, where another branch of the Kitchen family kept working Bedlington terriers at their farm, undoubtedly using them with the Eskdale and Ennerdale Foxhounds and possibly the Melbreak too.

The Kitchen's of Egremont certainly worked their terriers and they also kept a strain of the new type of Lakeland terrier which was given this name after a meeting at Keswick Show in the summer of 1912, breeding some of the most famous of the early pedigree Lakeland terrier breed, such as Central Grip and Central Midge. These early Lakeland terriers saw service at all large quarry and they were both game and sensible.

The Central prefix used by the Kitchen family had its origins in the name of the street where they lived, at Central Avenue on the famous Castle Estate, Egremont. Most of the early Lakeland terriers were bred in Egremont and Central Avenue played a huge part in the development of the breed until well into the latter part of the twentieth century, though even today Alan Johnston continues to breed the famous Oregill strain only a stone's throw away from Central Avenue where his grandfather, the famous Alf Johnston, established the Oregill kennels.

Breay and Buck's strain of what later became known as Patterdale terriers can be traced back to Central Avenue, through Myrt and Tear 'Em in particular, as Irving's strain of working pedigree Lakeland terrier was partly bred from Oregill and Central Lakeland terriers. Central Grip sired the incredibly good looking and game dog Vic of Wastwater, which is the ancestor of most modern working and registered Lakeland terriers, as well as Patterdale terriers. In turn, Vic of Wastwater sired Egton Rock of Howtown, a stud which bred many excellent show and working Lakeland terriers. Egton Rock, in fact, was a prolific sire of workers and his progeny found a ready market all over the fells, as they were both game and narrow enough to get anywhere.

Alf Johnston (right) & Billy Ridley exhibiting registered Lakeland terriers which influenced Breay's breeding programme

Central Grip also sired Central Midge and she in turn was the dam of the famous Scawfell Guide who was also owned by the Kitchen family of Egremont and used, not only for winning extensively at shows staged throughout the Lakes, but also for working all large quarry, the most noted of which was badgers. Kitchen's terriers were used on badger digs around Egremont and beyond and they acquitted themselves well. So well, in fact, that Willie Irving had no qualms about bringing the Central strain into his breeding programme, so it seems unlikely that Tommy Dobson would have had any objections to using the Kitchen bred Bedlingtons on his strain, and perhaps also their crossbred strain of fell, or coloured, working terrier long before 1912 (Dobson died in 1910 after catching a chill whilst hunting in the Langdales) when the new, better looking type was given the name of Lakeland terrier.

Bedlington terriers were also still quite popular with some breeders during the first half of the twentieth century and 'Mowdie'

Robinson who lived at Hollins Farm, Lorton Vale, close to the Melbreak Hunt kennels, sometimes ran on and worked Bedlington terriers, one of which was named Rufus and he saw service with the Melbreak Foxhounds, particularly during Willie Irving's reign at the hunt (1926-1951). Robinson only tolerated top quality working terriers and Rufus lived up to his high expectations and was undoubtedly brought into Robinson's strain, which showed much Bedlington terrier influence. The 'Mowdie' Robinson strain may also have played an important part in the development of Cyril Breay's strain through Tink, a terrier used on his terrier breeding programme during the 1930s.

Breay bought Tink from a chap named Robinson of Maryport and he was a blue, scruffy fell type of terrier which was also partly Bedlington bred, as Breay told his son Robin that Bedlington blood had played a large part in his early breeding programme. Tink may well have been bred by Mowdie Robinson who did get about a bit and who had several different jobs, including stone chipping, grass cutting at Cockermouth Cemetery where he was an expert with a scythe, and mole catching. It is possible that Mowdie Robinson sojourned at Maryport for a while and at that time sold this blue dog to Breay.

Whatever the case may be, we can be certain of one thing; that Tink was very game. The fact that Breay brought this dog into his strain is proof enough of that. Tink mated Barker and it was he who sired Tiger, the bitch Breay gave to Buck after the Bishopdale rescue mentioned earlier. Tiger was obviously partly Bedlington bred and she had a slight brindling to her coat, which unquestionably indicated bull terrier blood not too far back in her breeding - something we will discuss more fully later in the book. Tink proved incredibly difficult to break to sheep (a lack of proper training in puppyhood, likely before Breay purchased the dog) and so Breay gave the dog to Frank Buck.

Tiger became a superb worker when used both privately and with hounds. One day she worked a fox put in by the Bedale Foxhounds and a few hunt terriers were tried, but this fox refused to bolt and it bettered each one. Frank Buck was asked to try Tiger and she got stuck into her fox and succeeded in bolting it, which so impressed

Major Burdon (the Master) that he asked Buck if he would allow his crossbred border/fell terrier to mate this bitch. Frank obliged and this union produced Blitz; a terrier which was supposedly the first of the strain to have a massive head with steel-trap jaws, but powerful headed terriers appeared in the strain before this time.

Roger Westmorland (right) with a Breay-bred Patterdale terrier

High Lea Laddie is one of the ancestors of Breay's strain (early 1930s)

For instance, I have in my possession a poor quality photograph taken during either the late 1930s or possibly at the beginning of the 1940s showing Breay with a black terrier with a massively powerful head. This terrier must have been bred before Blitz came on the scene, though without question Blitz was one of the most important stud dogs in Breay and Buck's strain and he had a huge influence on breeding policy. This terrier in the photograph could not be Blitz, as Blitz was the colour of a Border terrier, not black.

By this time (1940) Sealyham, Bedlington, the old type of Patterdale terrier, and fell or coloured working terrier blood had all gone into the mix and that mating between Tiger and the Major Burdon stud dog had introduced good quality Border terrier blood into the mix too. That mating in 1940 also saw the beginning of the Breay/Buck breeding programme, but make no mistake, it was Cyril Breay who laid the foundation stones for a strain of terrier that would become known as the Patterdale terrier and which would increase massively in popularity during the twenty-first century in particular. That rescue in Bishopdale cemented a lifelong breeding programme and that litter born to Tiger in 1940 remains one of the most important unions in working terrier history. What a massive influence Breay's Tiger had on the strain after she had so successfully worked that fox out of a bad place with the Bedale Foxhounds. Such excellent working qualities had resulted from Breay's selective breeding programme, putting the very best working dogs to the very best working bitches.

8. BREAY'S RUBY & GEM

Cyril Breay's Gem was quite simply one of the strongest and gamest of terriers ever to have gone to ground. She was a big, bold, powerful bitch terrier and her prowess as a finder and worker of foxes made her a legend in her own lifetime. She saw much service working privately for farmers and gamekeepers alike and she was tested in a variety of earths which were located in different areas around the country, most notably in Cumbria, North Yorkshire, Southern Scotland, Lancashire and Lincolnshire. She also worked the deep and difficult earths of the Western Pennines, particularly around Bolton and Chorley where John Fithian, a Lancashire farmer, hosted plenty of visits by Breay. Fred Jenkinson lived at Wray and he would often take Breay hunting around Chorley and

Bolton along with Neville Chatwood, who also kept Breay's strain of terrier. But it was working the vast, dangerous earths of Limestone country where Gem really made a name for herself, particularly while serving with the Lunesdale Foxhounds, for whom she did much grand work.

Cyril Breay with Gem (left) & Skiffle in his garden at High Casterton

Gem was born during the early 1950s and she was sired by Monty, a famous worker who was a grandson of Tiger, the bitch Breay gave to Frank Buck after he had helped rescue her and her dam, Barker, from a bad place in Bishopdale during the 1930s; a rescue which cemented the Breay/Buck lifelong friendship – a friendship which produced some of the best working terriers ever bred and, of course, the foundation stock of the modern Patterdale terrier.

The dam of Gem was Ruby, a chocolate bitch sired by Walter Parkin's Rock, yet another famous worker who was a grandson of Albert Benson's Red Ike. Rock was in turn sired by a terrier from the Breay/Buck breeding programme, as Walter Parkin was very impressed by the working abilities of this strain, more especially after he had seen Barker and Tiger work and finish a fox in that vast Bishopdale rock-pile. Red Ike served with both the Blencathra and Coniston Foxhounds and he ran loose with hounds. He was a big terrier, sixteen inches at the shoulder, yet he worked several vast borrans and killed or bolted many, many foxes for both packs. Ruby was another incredibly game bitch, which, I suppose, isn't in the least surprising, when one considers her breeding. In fact, it may well be said that Ruby was too game. She was a hard bitch at fox, but one day, while working a rock-pile in an old quarry situated on the fells between Hutton Roof and Burton-in-Kendal, Ruby switched her attentions to a badger and she tackled it as she would a fox. Tragically, poor Ruby had her throat torn out by the badger and later died of her injuries (Robin can remember his father bringing her home later that day and the vet being unable to assist her). Before her demise, however, she bred Gem. Gem was possibly the first of the powerful, muscular, bull-terrier type terriers to appear in the strain, though black terriers had appeared in litters long before this. Certainly, there are photographs of Breay taken during the late 1930s or very early 1940s that show him with black terriers, though I suspect the black colouring had been a feature of the strain since the 1920s. Several of the early Coniston Hunt terriers were black during George Chapman's reign at the hunt (1908–1932) and Breay brought the Coniston strain into his own breeding programme during the very early 1920s.

Breay had undoubtedly spent some time following, and no doubt working his terriers with, this hunt (he courted and married a girl from Windermere and he may have lived at Kendal for a few years, where he was married). Gem was a first-rate working terrier in her own right, but she was also a superb brood bitch and Breay bred many great terriers from her, the best of which was possibly Black Davy, with whom Frank Buck won many shows. Another great terrier bred out of Gem was Skiffle. She too won many shows, but she was first and foremost a top class worker. Skiffle was probably a litter sister to Black Davy and was of very similar type. Davy was one-quarter Scottish terrier bred and when his coat was not stripped out the Scottish terrier influence was obvious. I suspect the Scottish terrier influence came through either Parkin's Rock, or the dam of Ruby, a bitch from Orton, as Scottish terriers did serve at the Lunesdale around that time.

Breay bred several litters out of Gem and she saw a great deal of work at fox in particular, but her abilities were badly affected one day while working a fox put in by the Lunesdale hounds, hunted at that time by the legendary John Nicholson. Nicholson was so impressed by Breay's terriers that he allowed Breay to work his strain with hounds on a regular basis, though Breay had also used his terriers when Walt' Parkin and even Tommy Robinson before him, hunted this pack. And so Breay was asked to try Gem after a fox had been run into a deep and dangerous ghyll earth at Barbondale – a ghyll situated quite close to the dale road. Gem was by then a legend and her abilities without question. True to form she followed eagerly in the wake of her fox, perhaps a little too eagerly in fact, for, while negotiating the almost sheer-drop sides of the ghyll, Gem fell several feet onto the rocks below and was badly injured.

This is a very bad place and was so deep that Breay, nor any other hunt follower could reach Gem and so she had to be left unattended while Breay could secure assistance. Even Frank Buck, an expert at rescuing trapped terriers, could do nothing for Gem and it took rock climbers and pot-holers from Settle to scale the sides of the ghyll with the aid of safety ropes. Gem was successfully hauled out of that grim place and went on to make a good recovery, but after that she never quite got things together again, having regular off days, and thus was lightly used at work from then until she died two years after her accident. Nevertheless, before her tragic accident, Gem had worked for several successful seasons and had bred many good looking and excellent working terriers. The Patterdale of today owes much of its good type and abilities to Cyril Breay's Gem.

A chocolate Patterdale terrier. It was probably Ruby which first introduced this colour into the strain

9. THE BREAY/BUCK INFLUENCE AT WORK

Old quarries are good places in which to find foxes and one day, before the Hunting Act had been implemented, my terrier, Fell, a dog terrier descended mostly from Breay/Buck stock, entered a rocky lair and quickly began baying. This was the back-end of March and my last outing (unless called out to deal with a livestock worrying fox) of the season, but I wasn't expecting much at this particular rock-pile, as I had never before known a fox to use this den, though rabbits were often found skulking among the passages between the rocks and I had successfully ferreted this place on many occasions over the years. It was immediately obvious, however, that on this occasion a fox was lying up among the stone-piles and Fell was now hard at it. Fell was quite a sensible terrier. Hard, true, but he could tackle his fox cleverly until getting in a fatal throat-hold and throttling his foe, though dealing with a fox in a commanding position was a little different. And, by the sound of things underground, this fox had itself a good vantage point from which to defend itself.

A working Patterdale terrier belonging to Tony Swift

This is why I have always liked a terrier, particularly a dog terrier, to have a powerful head with strong cheek muscles and jaws, as this type can best deal with a fox which has itself a stronghold in which to defend itself. My bitches have mostly been baying types and great bolting terriers, but every dog terrier I have owned, with just one exception, have been capable of finishing a fox that wouldn't bolt. Cyril Breay, co-founder of the modern Patterdale terrier, would never breed from a dog terrier that was not capable of killing a fox as such terriers were a must in the hard country he hunted. I have hunted in some of the areas where Breay successfully took hundreds of foxes and, believe me, some of the earths are very tricky places for a terrier to negotiate, let alone work foxes out of. When visiting such places, one very quickly comes to understand why Breay created such an incredibly game and hard race of working terrier.

As already stated, Fell was part-bred out of Breay and Buck bloodlines and was not unlike Buck's Tex in type, though generally of better conformation than Tex and possessing a more powerful head, which stood him in good stead in the rock holes and other difficult earths found among the Pennine Chain.

Fell was never a strong bayer, often working mute, though he had periods when he would bay eagerly and that is how things continued below ground on this occasion. He would bay for a few minutes and then fall silent for a time. It was obvious he and his quarry were not going to move, so I blocked the entrance with a couple of loose stones and headed off to fetch digging tools – a pick-axe, spade and bar. I also fetched Gary, who had also owned some useful terriers in his time and who had quite a bit of experience at digging-out foxes.

Fell wasn't too deep, but it was very quickly obvious that this was not going to be an easy dig. We made short work of the smaller stones which were mixed in places with a thick and sticky clay soil, but the bigger rocks were another matter and these took some shifting. In fact, some of the digging was back-breaking work and often the clay soil had to be dug out from among the rocks first.

Meanwhile, Fell continued on and I could hear him hard at his fox, as though he knew we were getting nearer and wanted to get the job finished before we reached him. I could tell this was a difficult place for him to work though and I was sure this was a big hill fox that was giving him more than a little trouble.

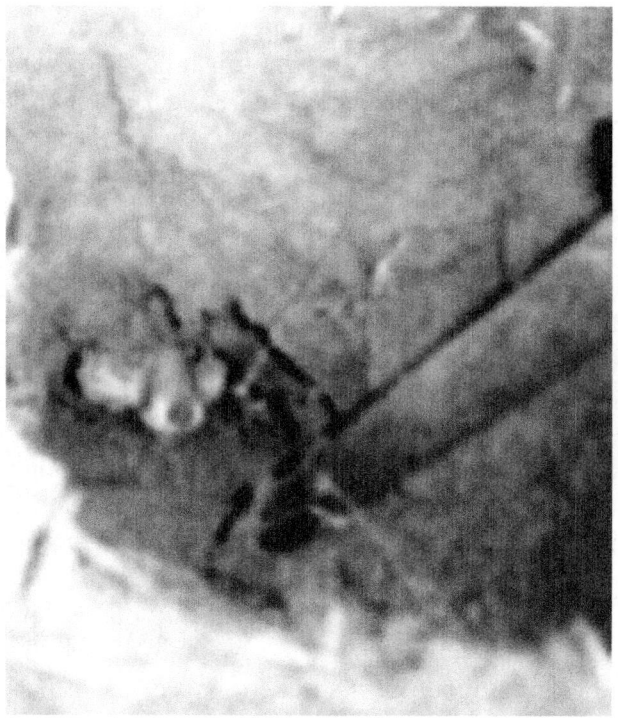

A fox at the end of a dig

I have read many times about difficult uphill earths where a fox can lie in a tight spot at the end and give a terrier a hard time from such a commanding spot. In such situations, sometimes all a terrier can do is stick with its quarry until dug out. As we progressed, it became obvious that this was such an earth. The rocks meant that the terrier's efforts to dig in order to make more room were futile. The passage narrowed as we cleared the rocks from around it and exposed the terrier's back-end, with Fell attempting to tackle his fox through a very tight opening. He now had a hold of his foe, but he could do nothing with it. It was obviously a big fox and he couldn't draw it, despite his best efforts. Thankfully, Gary had his fell terrier with him and we cleared enough space for him to get his head through.

Moss, a black Patterdale of the Davy type, grabbed hold of his quarry and at last the fox was slowly but surely drawn out of its stronghold, after a very difficult four hour dig. Fell was bitten more than usual, as he had the sense to avoid bad maulings in the main, but that was simply due to the fact that his quarry had gotten itself into a very tight and narrow spot that looked as though a rabbit would have struggled to get in. From such a place it could lunge at Fell, more or less at will. Gameness is measured in the determination of a terrier, however, and Fell had proven game that day. He had several difficult stints to ground, not only during the two seasons that he worked with the Pennine Foxhounds when Wendy Pinkney owned him (Wendy bred Fell from her own strain of working terrier), but during the several seasons he worked for me. This though, was one of his most difficult periods of work and such an experience demonstrated just why we need game, determined terriers to tackle foxes in the northern regions of England and why Breay and Buck always aimed to produce such game and useful stock.

10. THE RITSON & TYSON INFLUENCE

The original Patterdale terrier was not too dissimilar to the modern strains created by Cyril Breay and Frank Buck as early descriptions tell of hard coated, strong headed, straight legged terriers which were breeding true to type as early as the 1860s for certain, but probably for long before this time, and which were often red in colour. Although there were several breeders dotted in and around the Lake District, one of the most noteworthy was Will Ritson who, as was discussed earlier, resided at Wasdale Head in the Western Lake District where he also hunted the Scawfell Foxhounds. His terriers were particularly noted for their harsh coats, strong confirmation and general good type. They also had a reputation for being excellent workers at fox and other large quarry, though

Ritson's terriers also saw service hunting polecats and pinemartens which were a very real threat to livestock in those days.

Braithwaite Wilson (right) & Billy Ridley at Patterdale Show

Will Ritson was born at Row Foot Farm, Wasdale Head, in 1808 and was raised with hounds and terriers, as at least one pack hunted the area until he set up his own Scawfell pack some time during the first half of the 1800s. He was certainly hunting hounds in 1850, but had probably been doing so for some time before this date. This was a district famed for its terriers even as early as the beginning of the nineteenth century, so undoubtedly terriers ran loose on the Ritson farm and were used with hounds whenever opportunity arose. Certainly, by the mid-1800s Ritson, together with Willie Tyson of Ennerdale, had established himself as a top breeder of game working terriers that were being called Patterdales by the second half of the nineteenth century, if not earlier. Braithwaite Wilson, Whipper-in to Joe Bowman and Huntsman of the Ullswater Foxhounds after Bowman's retirement in 1924, kept a strain of hard coated quite typey terriers, many black and tan in colour, which he referred to as Patterdale terriers even as late as the 1920s.

Joe Bowman & his Ullswater hounds during the early years of the twentieth century

The truth is, Wilson was keeping the new, improved type of terrier that had been given the name of Lakeland terrier in 1912, his strain polished up with terriers from his close friend, Billy Ridley, and part of his foundation stock undoubtedly being from Mossop

Nelson of Patterdale who kept the old type of Patterdale terrier and who worked them with considerable success at the Ullswater meets. Wilson didn't like the new name for this type, though he undoubtedly ran on and bred a number of typey Lakeland terriers during his time at the Ullswater (1911-1914, 1918-1933), including registered Lakeland terriers bred by Mrs Spence at Howtown (Wilson used several of the Egton Lakeland terriers with hounds).

Tyson was another breeder of the old type Patterdale terrier and it seems that he and Ritson may well have enjoyed a relationship similar to that of Cyril Breay and Frank Buck, who used each other's stud dogs and swapped puppies, their breeding becoming intermingled until a predominant type emerged. Tyson's terriers became famous, not only for being extremely game and useful in the deep borran earths found at Ennerdale, Wasdale and Eskdale, but they were especially famed for their tight, harsh coats which easily repelled the worst of the winter weather. Just venture out onto the fells in bad weather in midwinter and you will soon understand why many of these fell hunters placed so much importance on producing hard, tight coats that could keep even strong, icy wind and rain at bay. While conditions can be milder, even pleasant down in the vales, up on the fells arctic conditions often prevail and you don't know what cold winds are until you have experienced such weather. For such reasons, Ritson and Tyson aimed to breed into their strain both hardiness and good coat.

During the second half of the Nineteenth century another noted family of breeders emerged on the Lake District hunting scene and these were the Nelson family who resided at Gatesgarth Farm, Buttermere and, later, at Patterdale. The Nelson family bred a hard coated strong type of terrier, up on the leg and very hardy, which could kill a fox that refused to bolt. Will Ritson's strain was the foundation for their breeding programme, which undoubtedly also included the terriers of Willie Tyson, for Mossop Nelson and his father of Patterdale, who both supplied terriers for use with the Ullswater Foxhounds, produced terriers with the exact type of jacket found on Tyson's strain, which were possibly of better type than that of Ritson's. The Nelson strain of Patterdale terrier saw much work with the Melbreak and Ullswater Foxhounds and they were famous for their abilities to bolt hard-pressed, reluctant foxes, or for killing those which wouldn't face hounds again. Some were lost to ground and during the 1860s a number of the Nelson strain were lost while working borrans in the Melbreak country, but nevertheless their influence on Patterdale terrier breeding at that time and even well into the twentieth century was tremendous.

Harry Hardisty, the Melbreak Foxhounds and Turk, bred from Willie Irving's terriers and ancestor of modern Patterdale terriers

Tommy Dobson used both Ritson and Tyson stock on his strain of working terrier and the Melbreak strain was also greatly influenced by such terriers. The Ullswater strain was also partly descended from Ritson and Tyson terriers and Coniston terriers too, had some influence from these dogs. During the latter half of the nineteenth century there was a strain of original Patterdale terrier being bred at Elterwater which served with the Coniston Foxhounds and one can say with certainty that such a strain was partly bred from Ritson and Tyson Patterdale terriers.

The original Patterdale terrier then went on to give rise to both the Border and Lakeland terrier after being crossed with other breeds and after being selectively bred until breeding true to type, but did the original Patterdale terrier have any influence on modern Patterdale strains?

The original Patterdale had a massive influence on Cyril Breay and Frank Buck's famous strain of terrier through earth dogs worked at the Coniston, Melbreak and Ullswater packs, all of which were descended from the original Patterdale through the Ritson, Tyson and Nelson strains of working terrier. Will Ritson seems to be one of the first to breed the original type that became known as a Patterdale terrier and it is partly thanks to his work that we now have hardy, good coated terriers which can stand up to hard work and the severest of weather conditions. Incidentally, Will Ritson's ancestors may well have been instrumental in the founding and development of the hardy herdwick breed of sheep.

Herdwick sheep are native to the English Lake District and for the past couple of hundred years or so have been the subject of great controversy; with regard to their origins in particular. Such origins have long been a mystery and it seems the early shepherds of Lakeland's vales wanted it this way. But if one looks hard enough there are clues as to where and how the herdwick breed of sheep became popular with the hill shepherds of the Lakes, and surrounding districts.

Legend has it that the Vikings first brought herdwick sheep to the Lakeland vales when settling in the area (their infiltration into the fell country seems to have been a relatively peaceful affair), but this cannot be the full story. I believe herdwick sheep are descended from flocks brought to English shores by Viking settlers, but I am also certain that the herdwick was not the original breed, but has sprung from those early flocks through selective and judicious breeding programmes implemented by shepherds of the eighteenth century – shepherds who were experts in their field and who knew how to get exactly what they wanted.

As far as I am aware, there are no records of herdwick sheep before the eighteenth century when William Clarke, writing in 1787, stated emphatically that the herdwick breed of sheep was created by shepherds at Wasdale Head, the place where the Ritson family resided, who were very secretive about their breeding programmes, which went on to produce a sheep that could thrive on very little and still produce hard-wearing wool and tasty meat. The herdwick was also incredibly hardy and could withstand what are classed as arctic conditions in winter as they clung precariously to the high places where they endured incredibly severe weather fronts throughout the year. These shepherds were so secretive in fact, that they sold very few of their new breed outside of the Wasdale area and so, before the mid-1700s, herdwick were rarely seen in other Lakeland districts.

Another Lakeland legend states that the herdwick was originally bred from sheep which survived the sinking of a few ships belonging to the Spanish Armada. These ships, according to this legend, were sunk off the west coast of Cumberland during the seventeenth century. It is hard to believe that this could be true, but this legend cannot be discounted, as circumstantial evidence actually supports it, giving this theory some credence. William Clarke himself was told by Wasdale folk that some of the sheep which arrived in the area during the seventeenth century were actually taken from a stranded ship that got into trouble off the west coast, which is only a few miles from Wasdale. It has to be remembered that some dismissed Clarke's writings as nonsense when they were published during the late eighteenth century, but he recorded his findings from what local people told him, so one cannot discount his conclusions.

I, for one, believe there is something in what Clarke wrote. If sheep were brought into the Wasdale area from a sinking ship during the seventeenth century, then it makes sense that, a few decades later, a new breed of sheep was emerging after the native breeds had been mated with the sheep from the wreck. Selective breeding could easily have produced a new breed within a few decades by expert shepherds and this would explain why, by the mid-1700s, herdwick sheep had become common in the Wasdale area in particular, but by that time were now being kept throughout the Lakeland valleys.

The attempts to keep this new breed in the Wasdale area by some shepherds failed miserably, as some who kept the new breed sold their lambs to shepherds from other districts. This went on until the herdwick was common throughout the fell country of Cumberland, Westmorland and North Lancashire and was well established by the time William Clarke carried out his investigations into the origins of this unique and hardy breed of sheep. So the next time you see a herdwick sheep, just remember the colourful and mysterious history of this breed, which remains common and well established throughout Lakeland, but which remains a rare breed outside of its native land.

Turk of Melbreak at the kennels, 1932, ancestor of Breay & Buck's strain

Douglas Paisley about to put a terrier (possibly Trinkett, one of his best workers at the time) to ground at Sosgill, Rigg Fell, 1930/31 season, with Blencathra Foxhounds. Paisley's strain influenced that of Willie Irving, which in turn influenced Breay & Buck's breeding programme

11. THE QUESTION OF BULL TERRIER BLOOD

One of the most hotly debated questions among terrier enthusiasts, even today, is whether or not Cyril Breay and Frank Buck used bull terrier blood on their strain of working terrier. Both Cyril Breay and Frank Buck denied that they ever used bull terrier blood on their strain of terrier, but it must be noted here that Frank Buck, as I revealed in my book *The Patterdale Terrier* (first published in 2004), at one time either ran on, or borrowed, a male pied Staffordshire bull terrier which he used for holding badgers at the end of a dig. This bull terrier was certainly game, but was as keen to latch onto Border terriers owned by Major Williams, the host of organised badger digs which were attended by both Breay and

Buck, as he was the badgers themselves. This bull terrier, in fact, was such a problem that Mrs Williams asked Cyril Breay not to bring Frank Buck again if he insisted on bringing "that dog."

Did Breay and Buck use this dog on one of their bitches? Alternatively, did an associate of Buck own the dog and use it on one of their bitches, with Breay and Buck using perhaps a bull terrier/fell cross on their strain? On reflection, I believe they may well have used a half-bred, or one-quarter bred bull/fell cross on selected bitches to improve bone, jaw strength and gameness in their terriers. This does not mean that I am accusing Breay and Buck of being dishonest. Far from it, in fact, as a crossbred would not be regarded as a bull terrier. Breay was a very truthful man and I do not doubt that if he had put a pied bull terrier to one of his bitches he would simply have said so. But if he used a crossbred partly bred out of bull terrier stock, then he could honestly state that he had never put a bull terrier to any of his bitches. Buck, although a keen "tourist baiter" or, to use a more modern phrase, a 'wind-up merchant,' I am sure would have admitted using a bull terrier on his bitches. One thing is certain; Frank Buck did use a pied bull terrier for a period of time which was very likely on loan, probably being tested for gameness before someone, possibly an associate of Buck, brought such blood into their strain. A puppy from the union, or even a grandson or granddaughter, may then have been used on Breay and Buck's strain, as type from the 1950s onwards, seemingly beginning with Breay's Gem, indicated that Bull terrier blood had indeed gone into the mix around, or before, that time.

Looking at the pedigree of Breay/Buck bred terriers only one bitch stands out as a possible link to that pied bull terrier (none of the dog terriers could have been bred out of that bull terrier). This is the bitch from Tebay of unknown breeding who was the mother of Breay's Ruby, who was in turn the mother of Gem. Ruby was the first of the chocolate coloured terriers to appear in the strain. Ruby was certainly incredibly game and she proved to have no reverse gears, which can indicate bull terrier breeding. Ruby died after having her throat torn out by a badger skulking in rocks at an old quarry, which she had tackled head on, in the same way she tackled foxes. Breay managed to dig her out and she was just about alive, but he couldn't allow her to suffer any longer, so he had the vet put her down that evening. Could that mother of Ruby have been a daughter of that pied bull terrier, or even a granddaughter? Another possibility is a red bitch from Orton which was the mother of Breay's famous Monty, who was bred during the war and who was named after General Montgomery. Breay's Blitz was the sire of Monty.

Cyril Breay & Roger Westmorland with Patterdale terriers of a type which first began to appear during the early 1950s

It is very likely however that this red bitch from Orton was bred out of Walter Parkin strain fell terriers, though she may well have been bred by either Buck or Breay. Walter Parkin was then hunting the Lunesdale Foxhounds which were kennelled at Orton (they moved to new kennels at Cautley after John Nicholson became Huntsman) and so this bitch was likely one of his breeding. Walt' Parkin was a very skilled stonemason and builder and he played a huge part in constructing and maintaining the kennels at Orton. Walter then went on to firmly establish the Lunesdale Foxhounds as a great pack which famously worked-out fox drags for hours at a time, successfully hunting and catching many foxes after doing so, with much longer hunts being the norm in those days. During one season he accounted for 103 foxes with his hounds and terriers, which was an incredible achievement when foxes were far fewer in number than in more modern times. Photographic evidence proves that he kept black terriers too and these were no doubt bred out of Breay stock.

One such hunt on Leck Fell ended in a fox going to ground at a rocky stronghold and two of his hounds followed the fox into the lair, but failed to re-appear. Walter crept inside and found what may have been an old mine, as hounds had fallen thirty feet into some sort of shaft. Walter was then lowered down on a rope and hounds were hauled out in old sacks, going on to make a full recovery after such an ordeal. Leck Fell, an area hunted frequently by Breay, is a bad place for hounds or terriers. Walter was a tough man, enduring long days on the exposed fells and walking incredible distances in the wake of his pack. He was also a superb terrier-man and terrier breeder, his stock being closely related to that of Cyril Breay in particular.

If I had to choose, my money would be on the bitch from Tebay, the mother of Ruby, being partly bred out of, or descended from, that pied bull terrier Frank Buck was keen to use at the end of badger digs. If this was indeed the case, then, yes, both Breay and Buck could honestly say that they had not used a bull terrier on their strain, as such blood would have been introduced indirectly through crossbred offspring.

Another means by which Breay and Buck bred terriers began to appear with bull terrier-like features during the early 1950s could well have been simply through close inbreeding. This means that several lines in the genes of this strain went back to bull terrier blood as far back as several generations. For instance, Bedlington terrier blood was introduced into Breay's strain during the 1920s and 1930s and it is a known fact that Bedlington terriers are partly bred out of small pit bull fighting dogs once common throughout the north of England and kept mostly by mining communities.

Early Dandie Dinmont terriers

These, crossed with Highland terrier type strains kept throughout Scotland, eventually produced the Dandie Dinmont and, later, the Bedlington terrier. The Dandie Dinmont of earlier times was a great working breed and they excelled at otter in particular. In fact, during the nineteenth century many of the northern otterhound packs were using Dandie-Dinmont type terriers with hounds and their courage and agility was without question. The bone structure and massively powerful heads of the early Dandie Dinmont betrayed bull terrier influence and it was this type that gave rise to Bedlington terriers after rag-whippet blood had also been been introduced to increase leg length when best-of-three rabbit coursing contests became popular during the early nineteenth century through to the early part of the twentieth.

It is true that such contests were more popular in areas of East Lancashire, West and South Yorkshire, but it is also true that Cumberland staged many of these best-of-three rabbit coursing competitions and two of the more famous establishments were the Pheasant Inn, Maryport and the Castle Inn at Bassenthwaite, where John Peel and Squire Crozier of the Blencathra Foxhounds occasionally enjoyed joint-meets with their respective packs. One of the contests held at the Pheasant Inn at Maryport was on January 1st 1852 and there were various entries, which were sponsored by the landlord of the inn, Mr E. Southwell.

Highland terriers which gave rise to Dandie Dinmont and all Scottish breeds of terrier

Twelve terriers were entered in the fourteen inch class and Mr Kennet's Nettle won, beating Mr Brown's Wasp. There were also twelve entries in the sixteen inch class and Mr Tunstall's Tosh, a well known terrier of the time, beat Mr Martin's Venus. There were eight entries in the eighteen inch class and Mr Tunstall's Tosh (he obviously had two terriers with the same name) beat Mr Ward's Pincher. Mr Peter Wilkinson judged the classes and the stewards were Mr Blackburn and Mr Hemerson. A large crowd gathered at the inn to enjoy the various contests and top winners like Tosh became local celebrities. This account gives us a fascinating insight into these competitions and such was the popularity of rabbit coursing that whippet blood was used to increase leg length on terriers even to the point of eighteen inch classes being staged. We tend to blame the Kennel Club for terriers being too large for getting to ground, but the truth is that rabbit coursing contests increased leg length on terrier breeds dramatically and even in the fells the working strains were affected. Just take a look at the old fell hunting photographs and many of the terriers featured were a good fifteen inches at the shoulder (Red Ike was sixteen inches at the shoulder).

It wasn't until Barry Todhunter, Huntsman of the Blencathra Foxhounds, pointed it out to me that I realised this. The fell-pack terriers are smaller these days, but at one time most were quite large, being up on the leg, and undoubtedly the popular rabbit coursing competitions were responsible for this increased size. It is important to know this, as Breay's terriers were often rather on the larger side and no doubt the ancestors of his strain were dual-purpose terriers – able to go to ground and tackle large quarry when needed, yet leggy enough to be used in rabbit coursing contests staged throughout the Lake District for a century or more (these contests became illegal, but were still staged in some areas, so some tales tell, until well into the 1970s).

Like the Manchester terrier which was simply a cross 'twixt black and tan terriers and whippets, so the Bedlington came about by infusing Dandie Dinmont blood with that of whippets, with just a dash or two more of small pit fighting bull terriers once common throughout the northern regions. Indeed, miners in Cumberland, Westmorland and North Lancashire kept these small bull terriers which they used for pit fighting, rat pits and fox and badger digging. During the nineteenth century and possibly into the early part of the twentieth century, many of the miners at Whitehaven and Workington lived in poor conditions and spent most of their free time in such activities, which were always 'spiced-up' with plenty of local ale that was cheap and readily available. Bedlington terriers were kept by such miners and unquestionably they became popular in the Lakes during the nineteenth century because they were not only extremely game, but were fast enough to be most useful at coursing rabbits.

The Dandie Dinmont also played a large part in the development of Border terriers and they even had some influence on fell terrier strains too. Miners largely kept such types and they took them to places where they settled after gaining employment. Many northeastern miners settled in the Lake District, along the west coast where mining operations were extensive at places such as Whitehaven and Workington, and they brought their rough-coated, hard-bitten Dandie Dinmont terriers with them, as well as Bedlington terriers. These were absorbed into rough and ready local strains and massive heads were produced in some descendants. In fact, many of the entries at shows staged throughout the Lake District at the turn of the twentieth century reputedly had large heads, which were commonly nick-named 'apple-heads,' indicating the use of bull terrier blood and possibly Dandie Dinmont blood too. So it is possible that Breay and Buck's breeding programme produced strong bone structure, bulky muscle tone and massively powerful heads through genes inherited from those pit fighting dogs which bred such terriers as Dandie Dinmont and Border terriers.

More bull terrier blood was added to Border strains probably even as late as the twentieth century (the huge heads on some Border terriers betrays this fact) and it is a well established fact that quite a lot of Border blood has been added to the Breay/Buck strain. For instance, Major Burdon's stud dog which mated Tiger in 1940 was a half-bred Border terrier. Another route by which Border terrier blood was absorbed into the Breay/Buck breeding programme was through the Border terriers belonging to Joe Dobbinson who was long-time terrierman to the Zetland Foxhounds.

It is not known if Breay and Buck took bitches directly to Dobbinson's stud dogs, but Jossie Akerigg certainly did and his terriers influenced Breay and Buck's breeding schemes to some extent, though it is fair to say that Akerigg's strain was largely influenced by Breay and Buck's dogs. Border terrier blood was obvious in Akerigg's terriers, which were similar in type to the Breay/Buck strain. I would not rule out Jossie Akerigg being the associate of Breay and Buck who used that pied bull terrier on his strain, the descendants of which being those that introduced more bull terrier influence into Breay and Buck's terriers. I say this because of a terrier Breay got from Akerigg during the 1950s, when he swapped a dog called Rip for Akerigg's dog.

This terrier was called Flint and Robin Breay can remember this dog, describing him as being "like a miniature Staffordshire bull terrier." He was rather on the large side and Robin said that Flint was "murderous at fox." Flint worked well for Breay and killed a number of foxes. Robin stated that the dog was very battle-scarred and he believes that Flint was one of the few terriers that his father lost to ground.

My research has led me to two known places where Breay lost terriers, one being the deep sandy holes of a place higher up the fell near 'The City' mentioned earlier, which was a very deep place, possibly leading into rock and where foxes got into such tight places that Breay's terriers couldn't always get to them, the other being a rock hole at Easegill, Leck Fell. One terrier was lost at this sandy place near 'The City,' but I doubt Flint would have been used in such a tight earth due to his larger size, so my money would be on the rock hole situated on the side of the deep Easegill at Leck Fell where Breay lost at least two of his terriers over the years. Breay certainly used Flint at this place, as he used most of his terriers there (Breay took many foxes from this earth at Easegill, including the last fox he ever shot). A farmer I was talking to while out with the Lunesdale Foxhounds could remember Breay losing a terrier in the sand hole located near 'the City' when he was a lad, but he couldn't remember which terrier it was (another farmer, an elderly sporting gentleman farmer, I talked to that day simply stated, "he 'ad some bloody good terriers, did Cyril Breay.").

The earth at Easegill was a huge and difficult lair which was usually safe to work. Indeed, Breay put his terriers to ground here and took foxes from it on scores of occasions as foxes mostly took shelter in a part of this rock den which was not dangerous for terriers to work, but, nevertheless, was not an easy place to negotiate. Breay was meticulous when hunting foxes and he would approach earths as quietly as possible, slipping his terriers in complete silence. Then he would wait patiently, as it usually took time to shift foxes from these large rock dens. The fox would often bolt from a fissure high up the crag where ravens nest each spring and Breay usually accounted for his foxes with a clean shot, though sometimes they did escape. However, on rare occasions foxes wouldn't bolt and instead headed into a shakehole adjoining this earth. Breay's terriers would follow their fox anywhere and very often they emerged safely from this shakehole (pronounced 'shak'ole' locally), but occasionally his terrier would fall into silence and never be seen again. Robin believes this is what happened to Flint.

Possibly, Flint followed his fox into the shakehole part of the earth, killed it and was unable to get out, or he may have fallen into the narrow fissure of an underground watercourse and been swept away into the deep recesses of the earth. Occasionally, though, terriers working in underground watercourses died from hyperthermia due to the constantly icy temperatures of these underground lairs. It is possible that Flint perished in this way.

Before his demise, however, Flint was brought into Breay's breeding programme and many terriers of today are descended from him. One of his most famous descendants was Jess, a black bitch terrier owned by Keith Clement of Kendal and one which was loaned to Anthony Chapman who hunted the Coniston Foxhounds for many years. Chapman was very impressed with this bitch and rated her as one of the best to ever serve at the hunt. Jess, after doing much good work with the Coniston Foxhounds and making a reputation for herself as an incredible finder and bolter of foxes, was put to ground in one of the huge rock-piles at Kirkstone Quarry after a fox had been run in by hounds, and, sadly, she was never seen again. Before being lost to ground, Jess produced at least two litters and her bloodline is still carried in many working terriers of today.

Robin stated that bull terrier blood was obvious in Flint, as it was in several of Breay and Buck's terriers. Could Flint have been partly bred out of that pied bull terrier used on those organised badger digs by Frank Buck? Possibly, though again one cannot rule out close inbreeding back to lines inherited from bull terriers decades earlier as being the cause of this obvious bull terrier type. One possible avenue by which this bull terrier type came about may well have been through a famous terrier which served at both the Carlisle and District Otterhounds and the Teviotdale Otterhounds during the 1860s – a terrier which may well have been one of the ancestors of the Breay/Buck strain. I also believe that this terrier may well have been responsible for the massive heads found on many early fell terriers such as Fred Barker's 'Chowt-Faced' Rock.

The Carlisle and District Otterhounds were formed when the Carlisle Otterhounds amalgamated with the Maryport Otterhounds in 1864, when they were kennelled at Catholic Lane in the City of Carlisle itself. William 'Sandy' Sanderson was appointed Huntsman and he took over from the famous Billy Robinson who had carved out quite a reputation for himself as Huntsman of the Carlisle Otterhounds. Sanderson, a butcher by trade, whipped-in to Robinson prior to being appointed Huntsman of the new pack and he freely admitted that he learned much from Robinson. 'Sandy' became an even more renowned Huntsman, but he also bred some outstanding terriers, though one of his best was bred by a joiner named Scott who lived close to the banks of the river Lyne in a district hunted by the Carlisle pack. This terrier was named Billy and he was a small pit fighting bull terrier weighing twenty-two pounds.

William Sanderson also hunted polecats and pinemartens and Billy was put to his first 'foumart' (polecat) when he was just seven months old, but he just played with it, which is not unexpected at such an age. The second polecat he saw, however, just a short time later, bit him and he erupted and killed it, as one would expect from such breeding. Billy never looked back after that. Although twenty-two pounds in weight and on the larger side for an earth dog, he could get to ground and follow otters into tight places among tree-roots and stone piles found at the water's edge, as well as drains used by otters fleeing from hounds. Billy entered to the first otter he saw, driving it from its holt when he was just twelve months of age from a place close to where Mr Scott, the breeder of Billy, lived. The second otter he was put to bolted and hounds hunted it into some woods where it was eventually lost, though Mr Standish's gamekeeper owned a bloodhound which found the otter the very next day.

A young Anthony Barker with two Ilfracombe Badger Digging Club terriers & 'Chowt-Faced' Rock, a terrier I believe was descended from Billy, the small pit fighting bull terrier owned by William Sanderson. The Breay/Buck strain was partly descended from Rock

Billy went on to become a famous terrier at the Carlisle and District Otterhounds and he saw much work, in spite of his size. This tells us that small bull terriers were often used in those days and that many of them could get to ground on large quarry. Such terriers would be used to breed further generations of working terrier and Billy would go on to mate several bitches, both in the Cumbria area and in the north-east of England, where he finished his days working for Dr Grant with the Teviotdale Otterhounds. Billy may well have influenced terrier bloodlines in the Dumfriesshire area too, where 'Sandy' often took his otterhounds hunting.

Dr Grant was a keen otter hunting enthusiast who hunted his own hounds in the wilds of Northumberland and the Scottish Borders, using Dandie Dinmont terriers with his pack, which he found most suited to working otters. Sanderson's Billy so impressed Dr Grant, who was a close friend of 'Sandy's,' that in the end Sanderson gave him this game bull terrier, though it seems that Dr Grant used Dandie Dinmont terriers almost exclusively. Billy may well have influenced Dandie Dinmont bloodlines during that time, as renowned workers were popular stud dogs.

The game qualities of Dandie Dinmont terriers made them very popular during the eighteenth and nineteenth centuries and Ned Dunn of Whitelee at the head of Redesdale was one of the most influential of the early breeders, whose terriers made a massive impact and which were unquestionably the ancestors of Dr Grant's working strain. Dunn's terriers were described at the time as being long in the body with strong, short legs and wirey jackets. They were quiet and shy, but were fierce when roused. Dunn's strain were closely related to that kept by James Davidson of Hindlee who may possibly have been the creator of what later became known as the Dandie Dinmont terrier, by putting local pit fighting bull terriers to rough coated, long-backed Highland terrier types.

One of the ancestors of all Dandie Dinmont terriers was Hindlee's Tar. Tar had a fearsome reputation as a worker, but Tar let Hindlee down on one occasion, which was quite a humiliating experience for him. James Hindlee was a gentleman farmer, or a statesman farmer, and he employed a number of people. His terriers had a bit of a dry spell of work and so Hindlee sent his shepherd in search of a cat that could be put to ground for the purpose of entering two youngsters Hindlee had bred. His shepherd called at Andrew Telfer's cottage and got a cat from there named Baudrons. The cat was put in a drain and one end was blocked, the drain running under the road.

Hindlee put his first young entry to ground and sure enough the novice terrier went like wildfire, but the cat almost tore the skin from its nose. Undeterred, Hindlee tried the second youngster after the first had had enough, but this was beaten off by the fierce cat too. Enraged and more than a little embarrassed, Hindlee then put Tar to ground and he was confident of the abilities of this bitch, but even she, after a fierce struggle, retreated and emerged backwards from the drain. Hindlee then exclaimed, "Confoond the cat, she's tumb'lt an e'e oot o' the bitch!" and his intentions were to throw the cat to all the dogs, but after digging her out she got away from Hindlee and onto a nearby wall and was then chased into a plantation by all the terriers, where she disappeared, no doubt climbing into the safety of a tree. Hindlee was forced to return home with all three terriers battle-scarred by the encounter and with the added worry that possibly his youngsters had been put off by this fierce tussle. Hindlee's shepherd called at Andrew Telfer's cottage later that day and there was the cat, curled up on a chair in front of the fire as if nothing had happened.

Dr Grant's Dandie Dinmont terriers proved very game and they excelled at otter, so much so, in fact, that 'Sandy' ran on one or two at the Carlisle and District Otterhounds (there is a painting of this pack which shows Dandie Dinmont-like terriers with hounds). During the 1860s this pack were hunting in Dumfriesshire when Swimmer, one of the more famous of the hounds, and Ben the terrier began dragging up the river. Hounds then roused their quarry at Cawhill and a long, hard, four hour hunt ensued, which culminated in hounds running their otter into tree roots where they marked eagerly. Another terrier, Randy, was put in and a fierce struggle began, but Randy was game and stuck to the task with gusto, eventually succeeding in bolting the otter which was caught by the pack a little later. The otter weighed twenty-six and a half pounds and was three feet eleven inches long – a rather heavy and fierce opponent for any terrier to face. Ben and Randy may well have been Dandie Dinmont terriers bred by Dr Grant, though that can only be speculation, as 'Sandy' also ran on fell terriers. Fox terriers were also worked with this pack and such terriers were used in the creation of the Lakeland terrier (Jim Dalton undoubtedly used Carlisle and District Fox terriers to improve type in his strain of Blencathra terrier).

Billy served Dr Grant well and during his time with 'Sandy' and Dr Grant he mated many bitches and unquestionably had a massive impact on strains of working terrier. I believe that Billy was used on Dr Grant's strain of Dandie Dinmont and that he was partly responsible for the massive heads appearing in this breed during the latter decades of the nineteenth century. And, through Dandie

Dinmont terriers, I believe Billy was instrumental in breeding many strains of modern Bedlington terrier. Not only that, but I also believe this dog influenced the breeding of Border terriers.

Bradley's Rip (left)

In his book, *The Fell Terrier,* Brian Plummer mentions a chap named Bradley who bought a Border terrier with a massive head called Rip from Newcastle Dog Market in 1900 and that he believed that this dog was the ancestor of the Breay/Buck breeding programme. This dog, according to Plummer, was responsible for producing massive heads and Bull terrier-like features in Patterdale terriers, as Rip was obviously partly bull terrier bred. It is my belief that Rip was descended from 'Sandy's' Billy and that this dog, as well as other fighting pit bull terrier types used to improve bone, jaw strength and gameness in other terrier breeds, may well have provided the genes which gave Breay and Buck's strain its characteristics. If Breay and Buck did not use bull terrier blood, or a bull/fell cross on their strain, then the only other explanation possible is that their close inbreeding programme produced several lines going back to bull terriers which influenced past terrier breeding schemes and by such means bull terrier features became dominant in their litters from the 1950s onwards. I have seen pied Patterdale terriers and I know others who have seen such terriers too, which could easily lead to concluding that such colouring and markings are proof enough that Breay and Buck brought that pied bull terrier into their breeding schemes. If only it was that simple. The problem is that pied colouring and other white markings found on many Patterdale terriers today could have come about via other routes, not simply through the use of that pied bull terrier, or other bull terrier blood.

12. WHITE TERRIER INFLUENCE

There can be no doubt that Cyril Breay started off with Sealyham terriers which he used for badger digging and fox and otter bolting in and around the Lune Valley area during his youth, as he grew up in a district rich in wildlife that would have given his terriers plenty to do. Legends of Breay coming north from Wales with his father and bringing with them Sealyham terriers are inaccurate, as Breay was born at either Middleton or Killington in 1891 or thereabouts, where Wilfred Henry Breay, Cyril's father, was the vicar. Mystery even surrounds the actual birthplace of Cyril Breay and from his birth onwards mystery seemed to have been a great part of his character. Breay's father was a busy man, as he was also the chaplain of a private chapel at Lincoln's Inn Bridge.

Cyril Breay was a well educated youth, but it seems likely that he spent much of his free time either fishing (his father was a keen fisherman, though Robin Breay has never heard of his grandfather being involved in any way with working terriers) or hunting. He undoubtedly had terriers or associated with those who kept and worked terriers from an early age, as his passion for working terriers must have been kindled early. He probably hunted with the Sedbergh Foxhounds as a lad and may have obtained his first terriers via a hunt follower, as in those days several breeds of terrier were still worked and my research has uncovered that cairn and Scottish terriers, as well as more typical breeds, did see work with hounds in the Lune Valley district, so maybe Sealyham terriers also saw service with hounds in that area. From whichever source Breay obtained his Sealyham stock, he soon set about seeking outcross blood and as we have seen he used one of the Coniston Foxhound terriers, a red dog of possible original Patterdale terrier type which was probably Anthony Chapman's Crab – a terrier which had a massive impact on working terrier bloodlines during the 1920s.

Harold Watson, at the insistence of Anthony Chapman, used Crab to mate his bitch, Fury, which he had obtained from Joe Bowman after his retirement from the Ullswater Hunt in 1924. Fury was one of Bowman's most famous terriers and was the bitch featured in the *Miner's Story* which told of how Bowman dug to her fearing for her life, only to discover she had killed three adult foxes during one session to ground. When with Harold Watson Fury entered a bad place and quickly and efficiently killed a fox that had been run in by the Coniston Foxhounds. This was during the 1924-25 season and Fury so impressed 'Auld' Anthony Chapman that Crab was mated to this bitch and she later whelped a litter of twelve puppies. This litter went on to make a huge impact on future fell terrier breeding, especially at the Ullswater Hunt. It is interesting to note that Walter Parkin first began keeping old Ullswater working terrier lines and that Breay and Buck brought Parkin's strain into their own breeding schemes, so Chapman's Crab, if not the red dog used by Breay during the early twenties to mate his bitch, Wendy, would undoubtedly have influenced Patterdale terrier breeding via this route; in fact, most terriers in and around the Lakes after the 1920s were bred down from Chapman's Crab - a truly wonderful and legendary worker.

The bars of Breay's original kennels are still to be found in the garden of The Thrang at Mallerstang where Breay lived from 1920-1938

Sealyham terrier blood is obviously partly responsible for white markings in modern Patterdale terriers, but it is also true to say that fell and Lakeland terrier strains were heavily soused with white terrier blood even during the latter half of the nineteenth century, so that Coniston red dog Breay used to mate Wendy would likely have carried genes which produced these white markings too. Breay had become very familiar with the Coniston Hunt terriers prior to 1920, as he courted and married Winifred Coots of Windermere in 1918. Breay had been educated at Cambridge and he spent some time before 1920 teaching at Repton Public School in Derbyshire and he also spent a little time teaching in Switzerland, which was likely shortly before he was married. He also taught at a school in Kirkby Lonsdale and lived in this charming village in a house at Town End that was long-since demolished to make way for the main road from Settle to Kendal.

The gate to The Thrang at Mallerstang, through which Breay walked every day for eighteen years. John Whaley, a Mallerstang farmer and enthusiast of the Breay-bred terrier, would hang sheeps heads on this gate from his father's butcher's shop for Breay's terriers

It may have been that he lived here for a couple of years after he was married, but records reveal that by 1920 he had given up teaching and had taken a house at Mallerstang called 'The Thrang.' From then on Breay lived the life of a country gentleman, spending his summers fly fishing and the autumn and winters shooting, following hounds and working his terriers; able to shun employment because his wife was provided for by a wealthy relative (Breay's wife was disowned by most of her family for marrying Breay, who was considered beneath her, but a rich aunt provided her with an annuity which the married pair could afford to live off).

Breay used some of this income for juggling stocks and shares and it seems he was quite successful in many of his investments, though Robin was quick to stress that his father never made a fortune from his shares. Wendy was one of his best terriers at this time and he hunted foxes on the fells around Mallerstang with this bitch. It was at Mallerstang that Breay perfected the art of tracking and shooting foxes and his only boast was that during his years living in Mallerstang he never missed a fox with his twelve-bore shotgun, which was an incredible feat. Breay was a very modest man who never sought attention, but he was proud of this achievement and told his family of his successful exploits at fox when living in this area.

Breay had the shooting rights on the fells east of Mallerstang, paying five pounds a year for the privilege, right across the bleak tops to Nine Standards which is one of the features of Alfred Wainwright's Coast to Coast Walk from St Bees to Robin Hoods Bay. He carried out his own predator control in the area and became an expert at hunting foxes with his team of game terriers. The earths in this district were mainly rock and peat earths and numerous times Breay tracked fox prints after fresh snowfall that often led to rocky lairs above the village, which can be clearly seen from the village road. He would slip an eager terrier and stand back downwind of the den lest his quarry caught a whiff of human scent, waiting patiently for Reynard to bolt. Sometimes foxes shot out of the earths like bullets from a gun, at other times they tested the air then slunk away stealthily. Every time, though, Breay took aim and if he didn't get the fox with the first barrel, he got it with the second. Not one fox did he miss in at least eighteen years of living at Mallerstang and hunting its wild fells. Having said this, at other times during his long and eventful life hunting the fells and other areas, he did miss foxes, but not whilst living at Mallerstang (Breay lived at The Thrang from 1920 until 1938).

Tommy Dobson with a white terrier, which may have been the ancestor of Metz. Notice the Dandie Dinmont type terrier on the rock above Dobson & the Irish terrier type to his right

White markings were common on Breay's terriers during those early years when he was establishing his strain, winkling out undesirable qualities and locking in those qualities which made his strain famous through judicious selective breeding. White markings were a mainstay of his strain, though he didn't seem to favour white terriers generally, as most were coloured. However, he once told Roger Westmorland not to have any reservations about using white Lakeland terrier blood in his breeding programme, as Breay had once used such blood with considerable success. This dog terrier he used as outcross blood was Metz, owned by Jack Porter, the son of Willie and father of Edmund, which served with the Eskdale and Ennerdale Foxhounds.

Barry Todhunter with a white terrier

It was some time during the 1940s that the Eskdale and Ennerdale Foxhounds were invited to hunt the Lunesdale Foxhounds country, which may well have been a joint-meet with the latter pack, and they 'loused' near Sedbergh, quickly finding a fox and running it to ground at a difficult place called 'Shiningstones' near Sedbergh. As one could surmise from the name, this is a huge rock den which had a formidable reputation as a place from which foxes couldn't be bolted.

Such places are often used by foxes simply because they can usually get out of the way of a terrier by either slipping into a very tight place or getting onto a shelf which couldn't be reached. Barry Todhunter once told me of such a place situated on the edge of Caldbeck Village known locally as Cat Crags. Both the Blencathra and Cumberland Foxhounds have run foxes into here and in the past thirty-odd years Barry could only remember one fox being successfully bolted from this stronghold. Broad How Borran and the "rubbish" heaps at Kirkstone are two more places from where foxes usually could not be bolted, though occasionally a terrier had been known to work foxes out of these earths successfully, such terriers gaining legendary status among fell-hunting folk. Foxes are far more agile than any terrier and they can squeeze into places barely big enough for a rabbit at times, so terriers have little chance of shifting them. True, a fresh fox, one which hasn't been hunted prior to a terrier entering its lair, may bolt readily, even if a terrier cannot quite reach it, but one run in by hounds would be very unlikely to bolt. Hounds ran a fox into Shiningstones that day and Jack Porter was asked to try Metz, though there were no expectations of success.

Metz had quite a reputation at the Eskdale and Ennerdale Hunt by that time and Jack Porter told his son Edmund that Metz was a "'ell of a dog." Edmund remembers hunt followers talking of the abilities of this terrier long after he was dead, but expecting him to work out a fox from Shiningstones was surely asking too much? Metz entered eagerly, as one would expect, and a few minutes later he began baying, signalling a find, yet still few, if any present, expected a bolt. However, Metz was soon to thwart their expectations as he bolted, not one fox out of that vast, difficult lair, but three, one after the other. There were literally gasps of amazement among the followers and included in these was Cyril Breay, who was so impressed that he asked Jack Porter if he could use Metz on one of his bitches. Porter agreed and thus yet more white blood entered the breeding programme of Cyril Breay. And, of course, through Breay's stud dogs and brood bitches, that of Frank Buck too.

Exactly how Metz was bred is impossible to say, but old photographs reveal that quite a few white-bodied terriers served at the Eskdale and Ennerdale Hunt even as far back as Tommy Dobson's era (1857-1910), but one of the most important of these was a bitch called Maud. This bitch was the foundation bitch of Willie Irving's strain and records kept by Irving reveal that she was a white Irish terrier which was serving at the Eskdale and Ennerdale prior to 1916, the year she bred a litter to another Eskdale and Ennerdale dog named Brant (Brant means steep in Lakeland parlance).

This pair of terriers began Irving's strain, but they also influenced the breeding at the Eskdale and Ennerdale kennels. Indeed, this pair of terriers, if not owned by Irving were probably owned by Willie Porter. It is entirely possible, even very likely, that Jack Porter's Metz was descended from the white Irish terrier, Maud. Irish terriers of those days did still come in a variety of colours, though red was by then becoming the dominant colour and one favoured in the show ring.

Large numbers of Irish folk settled in the west of Cumberland and Irish terriers were no doubt brought in by them, though Porter or Irving may well have obtained Maud from one of the Irish hunts. One thing we can say and that is that Maud was a useful worker, otherwise Willie Irving would not even have considered using her as the cornerstone of his famous and incredibly game strain of working Lakeland terrier.

When considering such a background of Breay and Buck's strain of terrier one can easily understand why it cannot be concluded that the pied bull terrier was used as outcross blood, simply because pied Patterdale terriers are not unknown today. Pied terriers were appearing in the strain as early as the 1950s, or possibly earlier, but that may simply have been due to Sealyham terrier blood and the outcross to Porter's Metz.

Hamilton Docherty (left) & Glaister. Docherty's terriers were partly bred from Willie Irving's terriers and Glaister's may have been bred out of Eskdale & Ennerdale strain terriers

A lot of the early fell terriers were partly bred out of fox terriers too, so that is yet another route by which white blood got into the mix. For instance, Irving's strain of Lakeland terrier was partly descended from early Lakeland terriers bred at or near Egremont which were partly bred out of fox terriers (I have documented proof of this). And records prove that Breay/Buck terriers were partly bred out of Irving stock through Tear 'Em and a son of Tear 'Em, as well as through Harry Hardisty's Turk, which was another Irving bred terrier.

However, in spite of all this, I still believe that Breay and Buck brought that pied bull terrier into their strain via crossbred descendants. The type, rather than the appearance of pied Patterdale terriers, which emerged during the 1950s, gives much credence to this theory, though that, as we have seen, does not provide conclusive proof. There is lots of evidence pointing to bull terrier having influenced the strains, but still, this matter will no doubt continue to be debated among Patterdale terrier owners for years to come.

Patterdale terriers ready for work
(Photo courtesy of Tony Swift)

13. A PUPPY CAUSES A FALL-OUT

Cyril Breay and Frank Buck, though two very different people, became firm friends during the 1930s after Buck had dynamited Breay's bitch, Tiger, out of a bad earth at Bishopdale, but as far as is known they only ever had one upset in their close and productive relationship.

Maurice Bell, the long-time Master and Huntsman of the Wensleydale Foxhounds, holds both Cyril Breay and Frank Buck in high regard and he says that Breay was a true gentleman and that Buck had a heart of gold. He commented on the close relationship Breay and Buck enjoyed, but could remember them falling out on one occasion over something to do with a puppy. My research may well have uncovered the puppy involved in this upset.

During the 1950s Breay and Buck-bred terriers saw service at the Coniston Foxhounds as Breay and then Buck had become firm friends with the Logan family (Masters of the Coniston Hunt), though Breay's associations with them dated back to before 1920. Buck had promised a bitch puppy to the Logan family and it seems that a dog belonging to Frank had mated one of Breay's bitches and that Frank had pick of the litter, which is normal practice if a stud fee isn't charged. Buck picked a bitch out which was to be sent to the Logan family for use with the Coniston Foxhounds, but Breay fancied this bitch himself and sent Buck a replacement puppy instead, keeping the bitch, which turned out to be Skiffle.

It is not known exactly how Skiffle was bred, but all indications are that she was sired by a son of Tear 'Em, a red dog bred by either Buck or Breay after taking one of their bitches to Tear 'Em (Eddie Pool of Patterdale can remember both Cyril Breay and Frank Buck bringing bitches to be mated to Tear 'Em). This son of Tear 'Em mated Breay's Gem, the daughter of Monty and Ruby, and produced Black Davy and probably Skiffle, though it has been said that Skiffle was a daughter of Davy. All the evidence points, however, to Skiffle being a daughter of Gem and a litter sister to Black Davy. It seems that Buck wasn't too impressed with Breay palming-off a different puppy on him and they fell out, but not for long. Breay gave Frank Buck another puppy too, Black Davy, no doubt as a peace offering and the friendship was restored. Of course, I cannot state with certainty that this incident was the one which caused Breay and Buck to fall out, but it is most likely that Breay keeping that pick of the litter puppy was the cause of strain in their lifelong friendship – a little glitch which was soon forgotten.

Cyril Breay (right) with Skiffle, winning Rydal Show in 1957. Joe Weir, the Ullswater Huntsman, is next to him with one of the Ullswater terriers, possibly a granddaughter of Tear 'Em

Cyril Breay did well with Skiffle. Not only did she prove game and a great finder in the deep earths within easy reach of his High Casterton home, but she was one of the best looking terriers doing the rounds at the shows during the late 1950s and early 1960s. Gary Middleton remembers this bitch well and he says that around that time there were three terriers that shared most of the prizes at shows staged throughout the Lakes. The first was Sid Wilkinson's famous Rock which was both a looker and a worker. The second was Harry Hardisty's Turk, another grand worker, and the third was Cyril Breay's Skiffle. All three terriers showed themselves beautifully, but, make no mistake; all three terriers were excellent workers.

Frank Buck also did well out of a deal which at first had upset him, for he was given Black Davy. Davy too, was a typey dog which won well for Frank, but again he was first and foremost a superb worker and a great finder.

Frank Buck with Black Davy, a show champion and excellent working terrier

Frank Buck used him with the Wensleydale Harriers at a time when farmers clubbed together to pay bounties on foxes accounted for in the Wensleydale area, simply because, after the Second World War there were far fewer gamekeepers and thus far more foxes which slaughtered livestock and which cost local farmers hundreds of pounds in lost revenue (at that time during a few months in Wensleydale farmers lost upwards of four hundred chickens to fox predation and Breay, Buck and Roger Westmorland hunted down the culprits, being paid for every fox they accounted for). The Wensleydale Harriers were never owned by Frank Buck, but were actually founded and funded by Donald Sinclair, the vet who was the model for Siegfried Farnon in James Herriot's books and who was even more of a character than Herriot's books portrayed, according to people who knew him and who worked with him. Sinclair hunted these hounds in the Wensleydale area, hares being their principal quarry, but often Sinclair couldn't attend (he hunted hounds himself and was Master of the pack) and so Buck would be in charge on those occasions, very often hunting foxes for the farmers in the area and Black Davy saw service with this pack, finding in the deepest of lairs and working out foxes from peat earths in the district. Buck also used this terrier with other hunts, such as the Bedale and West of Yore Foxhounds. Davy was a superb terrier in every way and one that became one of the most important sires of his generation, literally mating dozens of bitches. His influence was immense and most modern Patterdale terriers are descended from this dog.

Jim Dalton's Turk, c.1910, another ancestor of Patterdale terriers

14. A SAD ENDING FOR BINGO

Cyril Breay's Bingo was one of the hardest, gamest terriers to be produced by the Breay/Buck breeding programme and he was actually bred by Frank Buck, out of his bitch Topsy. Topsy was sired by Black Davy out of a bitch called Tallant and she carried one cocked ear, which was undoubtedly inherited from the Scottish terrier influence (Frank Buck's wife told Brian Nuttall that Davy was one-quarter Scottish terrier bred). Tallant was in turn bred out of Buck's famous Tex by a bitch called Tanner. Tanner was bred out of Mick, a full brother of Blitz, and Myrtle (this bitch could possibly have been Jim Fleming's Myrt which was bred by Willie Irving and used with the Ullswater Foxhounds). Bingo was thus bred out of superb working lines with plenty of Border terrier in the mix. He was sired by a dog owned by a chap called Robinson at Cockermouth and I strongly suspect that this sire was part bull terrier bred, as Bingo showed more than a hint of such blood in his colour and general type.

Bingo was a very deep chestnut red in colour and he was very muscular with a large, powerful head and a steel-trap jaw which betrayed a definite bull terrier influence in his breeding. His characteristics also displayed such breeding, as he was hysterically keen to get to ground and allowed few foxes to bolt, preferring to close with them immediately and tackling them head on. Flint, mentioned earlier, showed similar characteristics and he too displayed bull terrier influence in his breeding. Bingo, due to his hysterical keenness to get to ground, irritated Breay and he would often ask Robin to take the dog away from him, usually as he waited close to an earth for a fox to bolt. If the fox wouldn't bolt, then Bingo was usually entered in order to deal with it underground.

This was the case when Breay was following the Lunesdale Foxhounds and a fox was run to ground in the Lythe Valley, South Lakeland, which is famous for its deep peat earths. The fox wouldn't bolt and in the end Breay was asked to try Bingo. Bingo entered, found his fox and duly worried it below, but came out of that earth "absolutely blattered," as Gary Middleton put it who was in attendance that day. Although Breay worked Bingo privately with gamekeepers and farmers in the Cumbria/North Lancashire/North Yorkshire areas, he also served regularly with the Lunesdale Foxhounds and he may also have done some work for the North Lonsdale Foxhounds at that time as Breay and Jossie Akerigg began following the latter pack quite regularly during the 1960s.

The Scottish or Aberdeen terrier was once a great worker. Black Davy was one-quarter Scottish terrier bred

It seems that Akerigg had some kind of disagreement with the Lunesdale Foxhounds committee around that time and thus he and Breay often followed the North Lonsdale instead, though Breay continued to follow and work his terriers with the Lunesdale Hunt too. Akerigg was a superb shot with a gun and he tracked foxes, bolted or dug them with his terriers and then shot them, hanging their carcasses from his Garsdale cottage garden wall for all to see. Akerigg bred some wonderful workers which greatly influenced fell and Patterdale terrier breeding.

He was also an expert at catching foxes and that may seem a bit of a silly thing to say, but some people have a natural knack of hunting cunning predators much more successfully than others and Akerigg was of this calibre. The late Gary Middleton, who has bred some of the best looking and gamest Lakeland terriers in the world for several decades, had much praise for Akerigg's abilities to find and catch foxes and Middleton says that he took many hundreds with his working terriers. One day Akerigg was out tracking foxes after a fresh fall of snow and one set of prints led him onto the fells above Garsdale and took him to an old stone working, not really big enough to be called a quarry in the traditional sense of the word, and the tracks clearly led into an opening among the rocks where quarrymen of old had tunnelled in to get at the rock which was used for building farms, cottages and dry-stone walls in the area. No tracks emerged, so Akerigg knew that the earth was occupied.

Jossie preferred to bolt foxes and account for them using a gun, but this particular fox had itself a good vantage point and it seems that Akerigg's terrier couldn't shift it. True, he did have several fox killing terriers during his long and eventful life (one of his best was the unusually named Lasty, a powerful fox killing terrier which was a son of Bingo), but at this time he had good fox bolting terriers which did their best to shift this particular fox. And so he blocked the fox in and sent for Cyril Breay, whose dog Bingo had by that time become a legend, having served for five seasons with the Lunesdale Foxhounds. John Nicholson, the Huntsman at that time, had come to rely on Bingo more and more whenever a livestock killing fox would not bolt.

Robin accompanied his father that afternoon and they climbed to the old stone working, unblocked the hole and entered Bingo, who got stuck into his fox immediately, pulling it off the shelf from where it had dusted the other terriers and tackled it hard. A battle royal ensued and Breay feared for his dog, as it soon became obvious that Bingo was in trouble. Roger Westmorland, a friend of both Breay and Buck and one who still breeds this strain of terrier, was fetched and he went into the old working and fetched out the now-dead terrier and fox. Robin can remember there being no obvious signs as to what had killed Bingo and he and his father carefully examined the body of Bingo. They eventually found the fang of the fox stuck in Bingo's skull and undoubtedly this had killed him, causing a bleed on his brain which finally finished him off.

Cyril Breay's Rusty outside an earth. Rusty was a great worker and was a son of Bingo

That fox hadn't actually bested Bingo during the struggle has stated in *The Fell Terrier*, for Bingo, even after the fox had pierced his skull, had almost finished it off before he perished, which tells us that the piercing of his skull wasn't immediately fatal, but that he died suddenly while in the process of finishing his foe, his death probably being due to a bleed on the brain.

Roger Westmorland finished off the near-dead fox and fetched both carcasses out into the open. More snow had fallen during the time Westmorland was inside that rocky stronghold and the fells were generously covered in a fresh, virgin layer as they tramped back down the fell, Breay's heart heavy at the loss of his legendary Bingo. Cyril Breay lost few terriers during his long and eventful life, but Bingo may well have been the saddest loss of them all.

15. A NEAR-SAD ENDING FOR BREAY

Cyril Breay had a few near-misses during his long and eventful life and one close shave was when he was out hunting foxes at the southern end of the Lune Valley at a place called Quernmore, which is on the edge of the beautiful Forest of Bowland. Breay often went shooting in this area and he also carried out fox control there.

One day during the early 1960s Breay and a small group of keen shooting enthusiasts hunted an area owned by the Garret family and fox was the intended quarry. At this time Breay had his incredibly game dog Bingo and Rusty may well have been on the scene by this time too. Breay always kept a number of terriers, as many as between seven and nine at a time, so it is impossible to say which terrier he put to ground on this occasion, but we can conclude for certain that it was a good one, as this was a deep rock den and the terrier indicated to Breay that a fox was home.

Breay worked as silently as possible on these occasions and he quietly slipped his terrier, which rapidly disappeared into the darkness below ground. The guns stood around the place at the ready and it soon became obvious that the terrier had found its fox, which, having not been run-in by hounds or disturbed in any other way, quickly fled from the terrier, though as it emerged it cautiously showed itself at the entrance, having possibly caught the scent of one of the guns. An over-enthusiastic gun then took aim, but somehow missed the fox and shot Cyril Breay in the legs instead, causing quite severe wounds.

He was taken to hospital and was kept in for two weeks. A nurse he nicknamed "Silent Night" looked after Breay well, providing him with, not only first class medical care, but also copious amounts of tea. Breay, although not a drinker of alcoholic beverages, was a great tea drinker and he greatly appreciated her diligence in providing him with plenty.

On another occasion, Breay, ailing now with asthma and diabetes, almost died of hypothermia when he was out with a chap called Simon Hunter who hunted with both Cyril Breay and Frank Buck quite regularly. They were hunting in the Dales at a place called Gayle, where the Wensleydale Foxhounds are now kennelled and where James Herriot (real name Alfred Wight) often worked when tuberculin testing for Frank Bingham (Ewan Ross in Herriot's books), a vet who practised at Leyburn. In fact, Herriot spent much of his time working in the Gayle area when on his honeymoon with his new wife during the early1940s, tuberculin testing cattle.

Cyril Breay (right) out hunting foxes in the Ingleborough district with his terriers, the Batty family & Frank Buck? (centre) during the late 1930s

Breay may have been following the Lunesdale Foxhounds during a visit to the area, or he may have been hunting when he was a part of the fox control club which operated throughout the North Yorkshire Dales, but whatever the case he had a terrier to ground and was waiting for a bolt in extreme cold. In fact, it was that cold that Breay actually collapsed on the fellside and was only saved due to Simon Hunter's efforts to revive and warm Breay, plying him with brandy and getting him moving around. Breay survived the encounter, but during his advanced years he wasn't as hardy as in his younger days.

There are lots of hazards out on the fells and Cyril Breay had his fair share of problems. Robin Breay also suffered hardships while hunting foxes and he can remember on one occasion getting snow blindness while tracking foxes in the snow with the Leck gamekeeper Arthur Swettenham, an episode which made him really quite ill.

A successful day for the Batty family in 1936. The terriers were very likely bred by Cyril Breay

*Some of the crags at Mallerstang
Breay hunted with his terriers*

16. CYRIL BREAY'S LAST TERRIER

During later life Cyril Breay developed diabetes, which only served to worsen the asthma which had already afflicted him for years. Breay was a keen fly-fisherman during the summer months and once, at Barbon Beck, he caught over a hundred trout in one day, only giving up late in the day after an asthma attack forced him to head for home.

Although he continued to breed and work terriers until just a few years before his death during the mid-1970s, by the time of his death just one terrier, a dog terrier named Brush, was left in his kennels at High Casterton. Brush was a rough-haired red dog and he may well have thrown-back to the outcross blood I am sure Breay used from Johnny Richardson's Tarzan (a terrier Breay greatly admired), as Brush was certainly of this type.

Brush was a keen worker, but, unlike the vast majority of Breay's stock, was no fox killer, but would stay till dug out, though he was also a very good fox bolting terrier. Robin Breay probably worked this terrier more than did his father, whose health began to fail quite badly during the early 1970s. Breay then died in his sleep at his High Casterton home and was buried in the graveyard of Middleton Church in the Lune Valley where he had grown up and developed his insatiable enthusiasm for game working terriers.

The very last fox Breay shot was when he and Arthur Swettenham visited the deep and dangerous earth at Easegill, Leck Fell, which adjoined a shakehole and where at least two of Breay's terriers had been lost on previous occasions. Brush may well have been put in that day, or perhaps Rusty, Bingo's famous son and brother of Wally Wild's Kipper, one of the founding terriers of Brian Nuttall's strain of Patterdale terrier, before he was passed on to Roger Westmorland in whose kennels he ended his days, after Breay had become too ill to handle him. Whichever terrier went to ground at Easegill that day, it bolted a large fox, which shot out of a crag earth and climbed the fell, with both Breay and Arthur Swettenham missing with their first barrels. However, as the fox came round the other side of the crag Breay let go his second barrel and dropped the fox instantly. It proved to be a beautiful dog fox in full winter coat and Breay had the animal stuffed and mounted on his wall.

Steve Robertson of Tebay with a terrier bred down from the Breay/Buck strain

Before his father's sad death, Robin took Brush onto the face of

Casterton Low Fell which stands above High Casterton, and there Brush found a fox skulking in a drain. The fox wasn't for bolting, so Robin blocked terrier and fox in and went to fetch his now ailing father. Cyril Breay accompanied his son onto the fell, despite his failing health, and there listened as Brush bayed at his fox. Robin dug down (though once a keen fox and badger digger, Cyril Breay later relied on younger men to do his digging for him) right on top of the vixen and shot her, before back-filling the earth. This was the last fox Cyril Breay worked with his terrier, Brush, and, in fact, was the last fox Breay ever hunted. However, two days later Robin returned to the drain and entered Brush once again.

The game little terrier quickly found and began baying at yet another fox. Robin once again blocked Brush in and went to fetch the Barbon gamekeeper who helped him dig out the terrier and what proved to be a dog fox, which had obviously paired with the vixen taken earlier. Poor Brush later drowned, however, after falling into water while chasing rabbits, after Cyril Breay had died. Quite a few of Cyril Breay's terriers had sad endings. The fells are hazardous to say the least and the country hunted by Breay is literally honeycombed with potholes, shakeholes, swallowholes and old mine workings – death-traps to even the gamest of working terriers.

Some of the rocky strongholds at Mallerstang where Breay worked his terriers from 1920-1938

17. TIPS ON CHOOSING A PUPPY & A NAME

Choosing a puppy should be a pleasure, and one to be savoured slowly. Never rush into a decision and if a breeder is constantly trying to pressure you into making one, then it may be best to walk away from the deal. A decent breeder will be more than happy to allow you time to choose a puppy, as a decision can be difficult to reach, especially if you are among the first to view a litter and a bundle of lovely puppies are crawling all over you for attention. A good breeder should be more than happy to provide potential buyers with a cup of tea or coffee while they take some time to come to a final decision.

What to Look for in a Puppy

Good health more or less sums up what to look for in a puppy, but there is a lot that goes along with this. For instance, it is always best to buy from a breeder with a good reputation, though someone who breeds an occasional litter should not be overlooked, as they may have just what you are looking for.

Do not go off outward appearances either. The house may look scruffy as you approach, but it may still be worth having a look at the litter. If the puppies and nursing bitch are obviously not healthy, then walk away. If the house is scruffy, but the puppies and dam are healthy, active and alert, then why not have a good look? After all, some folk look after their dogs far better than they do their houses, or even themselves.

The puppies you look over should be active and in obvious good condition. If you come across a sickly litter and the breeder excuses them by saying they are a little unwell as he has just wormed them, or some similar excuse, then do not close the deal, walk away and look elsewhere instead.

A puppy should have bright eyes, a glossy sheen to the coat, with no bald patches, or rashes on the skin. When looking at a litter have a look around the belly area and along the back. If there are red patches in the skin, then the puppy has a skin condition. Look out for these red patches, or even scabs, under the fur too, as a puppy with a skin condition could end up costing you a fortune in veterinary treatment. Pinch the skin together along its back, but not with any force so that you hurt the puppy. When you let go of the skin it should go back into place quickly. If not, then the puppy is likely to be dehydrated. This could be indicative of some health problem, such as diarrhoea. You cannot usually check the motions of puppies as the bitch, even at eight weeks of age; the minimum age puppies should be parted from their dam, will likely eat them immediately, in order to keep their environment as clean as possible. A bitch which is diligent in this regard will go a long way to preventing diseases among the litter, and especially the outbreak of stomach bugs, which can cause havoc among young puppies if left unchecked (a problem known as 'scouring' among country folk).

A Patterdale terrier puppy bred by the author

If you do take a little time, you may be present when the puppy you are interested in defecates, or urinates. Make certain the motions are not runny and that the puppy urinates normally. The eyes should be both bright and clean. Some books state that noses should be cold and wet, but that is not a reliable indication of good health in a puppy, or an adult dog for that matter. There are times when the nose can be dry and warm, but this is normal, as long as the nose returns to being cold and wet and the puppy or adult dog does not show any signs of sickliness.

Making a Choice

It is true to say that puppies differ in temperament and personality; some can be bold, approaching you and playing happily, while others may be a little reluctant. If a puppy is reluctant to approach you or your children, do not write it off; if this one appeals to you and your children in other ways. However, if the puppy is a trembling nervous wreck, then it is best to leave that one well alone. Choose the puppy that appeals to you, or, better still, allow your children to do the choosing. If possible though, go to view a litter without the children first of all. This can more easily be done if a litter is local and if the breeder will allow you a second viewing with your children, which any decent breeder would be happy to do.

This allows you to avoid possible broken hearts among your children. If they love one of the puppies, but it is obviously sickly, or the whole litter is not suitable, then you will have to walk away and this could mean great disappointment to 'kiddies.' If a litter is not local, then your wife/husband or a friend could go along and supervise the children in the car, while you have a quick look over the litter. If suitable, the children can then be asked in. This method could thus save much heartache.

Children and dogs often share some sort of mysterious affinity and a puppy chosen by children and reared with children often grows into a very well-adjusted and agreeable animal with plenty of personality. Patterdale terriers already have plenty of personality, but one brought up in a family environment seems to develop that extra-special something that cannot be explained. If you take your children along to view a litter, and you must, then allow them to handle the litter and play with them. Keep an eye on them, of course, making certain they are gentle with the youngsters, but by doing this you will have plenty of time to observe the litter closely. Many Patterdale terriers have great personalities which make them ideal family pets, as well as great working dogs, and that is no accident. The main breeders of this type of terrier were almost all family men, including Cyril Breay, so it was imperative that their charges were good with children.

If you cannot carry out a first viewing alone, do not allow children to go straight to the puppies and make a choice, as you must first make certain all are healthy and free of skin problems or any other obvious complaints. Also, and this is most important, make certain that a bitch is happy to have her puppies handled (most bitches are happy to have their puppies handled long before they are eight weeks of age). If not, then she should be put out of the room while her litter is viewed. Once you have decided a litter is suitable then you should encourage your children to make their choice. If a breeder will not allow you sufficient time for this, then do not rush in and purchase a puppy. Make it clear that you need to look them over carefully *before* making a choice.

Have a look in the ears and make sure they are clean. Allow for a little wax here and there, but if the ears are full of wax and black bits everywhere, it is likely they have either canker, or ear mites, or possibly both. Puppies which look thinly fleshed, with large pot bellies, are sure to be full of worms. Dirty ears and pot bellies usually accompany one another. This is a neglectful breeder who should not be dealt with. The dam will also be full of worms and will have been throughout pregnancy and rearing, so keep well clear of these sickly puppies, which will likely grow into sickly adults. You will likely never be away from the vets if you purchase such a puppy, which will probably cost you the equivalent of a second mortgage! A good breeder will have wormed the puppies at least a couple of days before beginning to sell his litter.

Purchasing, Transportation & the New Home

If all is well health-wise and one of the puppies appeals to you and your family, then seal the deal. A good sturdy cardboard box with newspaper in the bottom will be ideal for transporting the puppy home. It is best not to allow your children, or anyone else for that matter, to hold the puppy while on the move, as an accident, or having to brake sharply, could kill or injure the youngster. It will be much safer in a sturdy box placed on the floor in front of the passenger seat.

Before leaving the seller's home ask if you can take a small amount of the bedding from the whelping box with you, which will have all of the scents of the dam and litter on it, thus comforting the puppy for a day or two until it gets more familiar with its new home. It is also good to ask for a small amount of food, so that you can mix it with the food you will be using, which method cuts down considerably on stomach upsets. This is not essential, as a puppy will soon get settled with a new diet, but a steady change of feed is always the best option.

The Future Worker

If you are choosing a puppy with work in mind, then it is always the wisest option to purchase stock from working bloodlines. There are plenty of reputable breeders of working Patterdale terriers and these can quite easily be found through the pages of publications such as *The Countryman's Weekly,* or on facebook pages and other sites on the internet. When working terriers it is always best to be familiar with the laws of the land of the country in which you live and to do your best to work your terriers within these laws.

If coat type is an issue, then it is wise to ask to see both parents, if at all possible, so that you can check on the jackets. If both have good coats, then likely the puppies will have too, though there are no guarantees. The best chance of getting a puppy with a good coat though, is to buy one whose parents have tight, harsh jackets. However, many Patterdale terriers are smooth coated.

The eventual size of a terrier, an important matter when it comes to working stock, is also difficult to ascertain, but if both parents are of a decent size for work and are of a size to be spanned properly, then it is likely that their offspring will not be too big either. If a puppy has massive paws, then it will undoubtedly grow to be of a larger size, but small paws on a puppy will indicate that it will not usually grow too big. A terrier that grows too big for many earths, however, can still be very useful for bushing work, if that is your preference.

Settling in the New Puppy

Puppies differ in temperament and some settle in almost immediately, while others take a day or two to respond to their new environment. If your puppy is a bit sulky, then by all means nurse it on your lap until it becomes a little bolder and more comfortable, but if it is boisterous and untroubled by the journey and new surroundings, then by all means play with the puppy. However a puppy responds to its new home and owners, it will only take a day or two to become more settled, quickly finding its place in the family arrangement. One tip to helping your puppy settle is to give it a light feed soon after getting it home. I have found that this does help a puppy to feel more settled.

A young Patterdale terrier belonging to Tony Swift

Choosing a Suitable Name
The first thing to do after purchasing a new puppy is to give it a name, as becoming familiar with its name is essential to socialising

and training. It can be a good thing to allow children to name their new pet, but be prepared for a name that you would usually never even consider. A friend of mine had a chocolate coloured terrier and he asked his children to name her, which they did. 'Biscuit' was how she became known and that, surely, was always going to be the obvious choice.

Many Patterdale terriers have unusual names and I often name mine after Lakeland features such as a crag, or I use traditional Lake District names such as Turk or Mist. There are a whole host of other names, mostly originating in the Lakes, that are given to this breed and there is an extensive list at the back of this book which you may find helpful.

Whatever name you or your children choose, make certain it trips off the tongue comfortably and suits your terrier, as it will be stuck with it for the next decade and more. It is important to get the naming of terriers right, as it is not a good idea to change a name once the puppy has got familiar with it and is responding to its name; this would only cause confusion and confusion makes a dog unsettled and thus unhappy. Dogs need familiarity to be content and thus settled, so choose a suitable name and stick to it.

Harry Hardisty & his famous Turk

18. TIPS ON REARING, FEEDING & TRAINING

Allow the puppy to settle in for a day or two and then take it to the vets for its first injection, which should be administered at eight weeks of age (at the time of writing. It is best to seek veterinary advice with regard to all medical treatment). The last puppy I had injected was given its inoculations at eight and twelve weeks of age, which is different to the previous methods used on puppies in the past. Methods may vary, but your vet will advise you of correct dates on which to receive the second injection. Also, get your puppy micro-chipped as soon as possible according to your vet's advice. This is vital just in case you do lose your dog at some point, so that it can easily be found and reunited with its owner. Losing a dog is very distressing, yet it is so easily done. You just lose concentration for only a minute or two and your dog can have seemingly disappeared into thin-air, so it is always the best policy to micro-chip. It will become law in some countries to micro-chip in the near future, but it is because you care about your dog that you take such precautionary measures, not because the law tells you to do so.

The Importance of Early Socialising

Vets have come to realise the importance of socialising puppies as early as possible. Dogs which turn aggressive to other dogs or even people have usually not been properly socialised when puppies, so vets advise that, a few days after the first injection, once some immunity has built up, you take your puppy to friends and relatives houses where there are children and dogs. Better still, invite sensible friends and family round who have well behaved children and dogs and allow the puppy to play out in the garden, but not out on the street.

You must still be cautious and careful until after that second injection. Getting your puppy familiar with children and other dogs during those four weeks that a puppy isn't allowed out into public areas will do much to develop a good future temperament. Make certain, however, that such socialising sessions are always supervised by an adult. Children must not be rough with a young puppy, as this could cause later aggression. Older dogs need to be checked if they get a little too rough with a puppy too. A calm and relaxed atmosphere of playfulness and happiness must be the norm for a puppy, as this will allow it to grow into a well adjusted adult dog, though discipline is also important when necessary.

Young terriers should be socialised early on
(Photo courtesy of Tony Swift)

A couple of days after the second and final injection exercise proper can begin, but remember not to take the youngster on lengthy walks during those early days. Its paws must harden first of all, as they may become a little tender to begin with, especially after walking along paths and roads. The wide open spaces and encounters with other people and dogs may be intimidating at first, so short, but regular, walks are best at this time. Remember, wild dogs, as puppies in particular, can fall prey to predators such as eagles, or big cats, so it is a natural instinct to avoid open spaces where they are more vulnerable. That is why many puppies seem afraid to go on walks to begin with, but experience will teach them that they are perfectly safe and then they will soon come to relish exercise periods.

Those early walks are an important part of the socialising process and it is important to allow your puppy, while secured on a lead, to meet with other friendly dogs. You may wish to join a puppy group in order to make the most of socialising opportunities, but the same results can be obtained by taking your puppy to parks and other public places where there are friendly dogs, as well as into town where they will become familiar with crowds of people. The importance of such socialising cannot be stressed enough. It is vital that puppies get out among other dogs and people, particularly children, as soon as possible. Lead training is vital early on too, but we will deal with this subject a little later.

Feeding & Watering

Fresh water should always be available to puppies and adult dogs alike, and water bowls should be cleaned regularly, as a build up of germs can easily result in stomach upsets. Stomach upsets can kill puppies, so cleanliness with regard to both water bowls and food bowls is essential (make certain that all bowls are rinsed thoroughly after washing, in order to prevent any trace elements of chemicals being ingested by a puppy or adult dog). The hard work as regards feeding has been done for the dog owner these days, by manufacturers of complete dog foods which I have found to be excellent and very convenient when you live a busy life.

There are several good brands of complete dog food on the market, but do not conclude that the cheaper end are no good. I have used a cheap supermarket brand for a number of years now and it is both very affordable and very good, as my dogs thrive on it. There is less waste when using complete dry foods and my dogs eat grass and vomit far less than they did when I fed them brawn, or tinned meat, with a mixer. Their health is superb and that is borne-out by their eagerness to enjoy long walks and by their oily, glossy coats.

Use a specially formulated puppy feed until your terrier reaches the age of four to six months, as this will more easily be swallowed and digested. The first meal of the day should be one of cereal, softened with warm, not hot, milk (skimmed or semi-skimmed milk is best, as full cream milk can be too rich for a puppy. Alternatively, water the milk down a little). I give weetabix, or an equivalent, for the first meal of the day and the amount should be just one at eight weeks of age. The puppy food can be given at lunch time, then again in the evening. Just before bedtime, give a light feed of half a weetabix, which will help the puppy to settle for the night. If you are working through the day and cannot provide a lunchtime feed, then put in two weetabix for the morning feed.

A bowl of fresh water should be available at all times, but when a young puppy, do not use a large bowl that is full, as a puppy could fall in and drown. Use a small bowl with not too much water in, till the puppy has grown and such an accident will not occur. Remember to regularly check the amount of water in a bowl, as dogs, especially after being fed, will drink often. Make sure such things as mop buckets are not left around full of water (not to mention chemicals such as bleach and disinfectant). An inquisitive puppy can so easily fall in and drown.

Avoiding Obesity

Once a puppy has reached the age of three months cut out one of the meals, dropping to three a day. This can be dropped to just two meals at the age of four months, then one meal from the age of eight months (these are rough guides. Experience will help you to care for the individual needs of your dog). Of course, you may wish to continue feeding twice a day, but make certain that you do not provide too much food. Most dogs are greedy and will eat until they burst, so regulate their weight. An obese dog is an unhealthy dog. Likewise, an emaciated dog is an unhealthy and neglected dog, so always keep an eye on their weight.

A dog should look just right, which may seem a bit of a silly statement to make, but you will soon come to know the weight at which your dog is at its best. It should be well muscled and covered in enough flesh to avoid the bones protruding, but layers of fat should be avoided. Diabetes and heart disease will constantly threaten a fat dog, so if you notice your terrier putting on too much weight, then simply cut down on the amount of food you provide. This is also important when working your terrier.

Feeding the Worker

A fat working terrier will put much strain on its heart, but there is also another danger to consider. When going to earth a fat terrier can more easily become trapped below ground, as it tries to push through narrow places where it would normally be able to get if it wasn't fat. So a good working weight is one of leanness (though not skinniness) and muscle. If your terrier is one of the rough-haired variety, use your hand to check on the weight, as the fur can so easily hide the facts.

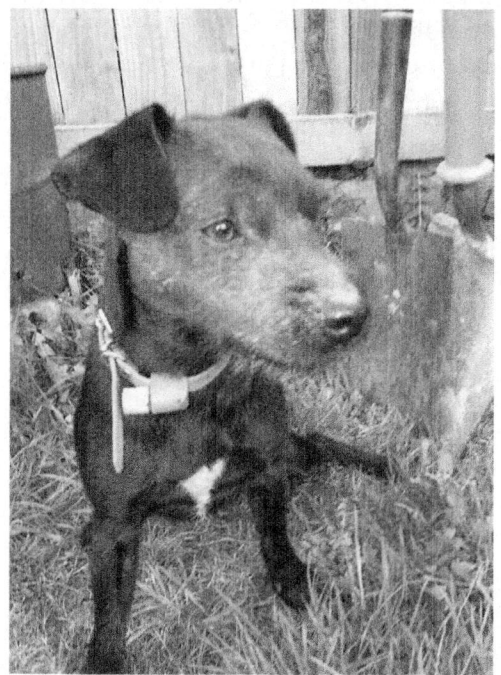

Do not overfeed the working Patterdale (Photo courtesy of Tony Swift)

Just feel the back-end and if the pin bones are protruding and the flesh is really sunken at the ribs, then increase the food until a more suitable weight is reached. The pin bones should just be felt on the hand when pressing on the back-end. There should be flesh around them, but they shouldn't be well covered. This is only a general guide to weight and you will quickly learn to regulate weight yourself, without advice from anyone.

If the ribs, pin bones and spine are protruding on any dog, then it is in a neglected and emaciated condition and needs to be fed much more (excepting old dogs, which can lose weight as they become more and more frail). I am sure most owners would never let an animal get into such a state and so keeping a close eye on weight, when a dog is both a puppy and an adult, is vital. Also, if an animal is fat, getting out of breath quickly and spending much of its time panting after any kind of exertion, then it is in an obese condition and having your dog fat is killing it with kindness, so learn to find a good balance with a feeding regime, remembering that a healthy dog is a happy dog.

House Training
This form of training is simple, but often the lesson takes time to be learned. Whenever your puppy urinates or defecates in the home, show it the offending mess and say 'no' in a firm voice, then carry it out into the garden while saying 'outside.' This must be repeated at every opportunity. Never allow a puppy to mess without punishment. This lesson can be repeated in a morning when you rise, as there will likely be a mess waiting for you. Whenever your puppy 'goes' outdoors, give plenty of praise, especially if it goes to the door asking to be let out. If, however, your terrier continues to make a mess during the night, it may be best to use a training cage. These are also excellent if a youngster is inclined to chew furniture when left alone. All-metal cages are best, as they last much longer than those with plastic trays. The confined space will usually prevent a puppy from making a mess in its own bed.

Basic Training – Come, Sit, Lie-down, Stay
The first thing to do is to get your terrier to come when called. I use a simple, but very effective method. First get your puppy familiar with its name and use it in such a way that the youngster associates pleasure with that name, so use it often when playing, praising and

stroking. Use its name when putting its food bowl down and, when it is out in the garden, call it in while shaking its favourite bag of treats. Milk drops for dogs are ideal for this, as they are both cheap and irresistible to a puppy. When your puppy comes to you, praise it and give it one of the treats.

Do this every time it responds when called and in no time at all it will associate responding to your summons with a tasty morsel. This can be carried on into adulthood, or stopped when your dog has grown older and is more readily obedient. It is entirely up to you if you will, or will not keep up the giving of treats when commands are obeyed. My own dogs grow out of needing a treat in order to be obedient and thus I rarely use them after puppyhood.

Training to sit is simple. Simply call the puppy to you and press down on its back-end while commanding in a firm, but not loud, or angry voice, for it to 'sit.' A similar method is used when commanding your puppy to lie-down. Put it into the sitting position first and tell it to 'lie-down,' while gently pulling out the front legs so that it has little choice but to obey. When responding to any command make certain you give plenty of praise and affection.

The stay command is a little more difficult to teach, but a puppy will soon learn. Get your youngster to either sit or lie-down and then command it to 'stay,' while putting your hand in front of its face. Repeat this firm command and only give praise if your puppy does not move. Remember to give praise while it remains in the stay position, not after it has moved, as this will only serve to confuse the trainee, for it will think the reward, or praise, is for moving rather than staying. Repeat these lessons as regularly as possible, but do not overdo things. Keep training sessions brief and enjoyable, playing little games after each session in order to instil pleasurable associations into your puppy.

This is vital. If a puppy grows bored and gradually develops a loathing for training sessions, then you will have done more damage than good, so brief and enjoyable must be your goal when engaging in basic training. Sit, lie-down and stay are simple enough lessons to teach and instil and these are usually enough for anyone who works their terriers, or who keep them as pets or show dogs. More advanced training is something I have never engaged in, so I would not even attempt to try to tell others how to carry out such training. Basic training has proved to be enough in my household and I pride myself on having well behaved dogs which are well socialised from being puppies.

Lead Training & Heel

Sit, lie-down and stay can be taught in the home and garden from as early as eight weeks of age, as can lead training. It is good to have completed lead training basics by the time the puppy has finished its inoculations and it can now be exercised in any suitable place. Lead training is very simple. Put on the puppy collar and attach the lead, allowing the puppy to drag it around for a short while, but not allowing it to chew the lead. Then pick up the lead and gently pull at it. You will likely have to drag your puppy for a while, but very gently, until it begins to walk in the direction in which it is led. Keep this up regularly while always offering gentle encouragement, but again keep the sessions short and pleasurable. Begin in the home, then carry on out in the garden and once inoculations are completed the lead training can continue at exercise proper. The lesson will quickly be learned and your trainee will soon come to love its walks.

Dragging a puppy gently is usually the way to get it to walk with you, but then a puppy can begin pulling and this is most annoying, yet is easily corrected early on. Simply jerk the lead, pulling the puppy back sharply, while firmly commanding it to 'heel.' This training technique must be implemented early in lead training and you must be both persistent and consistent in heel training, having your terrier walk at your side, not in front of you. Another helpful tip is never to allow your terrier to go through doors or gates ahead of you. You must lead your terrier, not have it lead you, which will help keep it submissive and thus well behaved. The young terrier will catch on in the end, though some take longer than others. I have never had a failure using normal leads and collars, so have never gone in for such things as choker chains and more modern designs to aid heel training, so I feel I cannot recommend them. If you are firm and do not tolerate any messing around, your puppy will soon come to realise this and it will obey you in the end, though be patient, as some do take longer than others to catch on. Another good training tip is to hold training sessions in different locations, so that the youngster becomes familiar with being obedient to your commands in all kinds of places and situations. It is good to train at home and in the garden, which are the most convenient places in this busy world, but public parks, out in the countryside, even in towns and cities, are other locations where training sessions can be held. Your puppy must become familiar with traffic, crowds of people, cats, other dogs, and, for those of us who enjoy walks in the countryside, farm livestock. There is nothing worse than to have one's dog chasing sheep or cattle. Not only is this very embarrassing, but it can be harmful to the victim, as well as your pet, as a farmer will likely shoot a dog that chases his stock. Sheep are very sensitive creatures and they can so easily die after being badly stressed. In-lamb ewes can abort after being chased by a dog, even if only for a minute or two. The milk of cows can be spoiled if the animal is badly stressed, so it is important to teach a dog early in its life that it must leave farm livestock well alone.

Breaking to Livestock
It isn't difficult to break a young dog to livestock, though if you purchase an adult that isn't trained in this regard, then it may be impossible to stop it from chasing sheep, cattle, or fowl such as chickens. In this instance it is best to keep the dog on a lead when in places where livestock will be encountered, though such an animal cannot usually be trusted anywhere as it will likely not only chase cats (cats can be encountered almost anywhere, in town or country alike), but will attack and kill them too.

This is yet another good reason for purchasing a puppy, especially if you are inexperienced when it comes to livestock breaking. It is child's play to break to farm animals with puppies. Simply secure your young dog on a lead and walk it among livestock. You could ask the farmer's permission to go into his fields with the animals, or simply train from the side of a country lane or footpath where the animals are plainly in view. Be careful, however, with cattle. It is best to train from the side of a country lane when it comes to large animals such as cows, as these can herd together and charge, especially if calves are in the field too. In fact, it is best never to go into a field where there are calves. Some horses can also be aggressive towards dogs, so be cautious with such large animals.

Cattle act according to instinct, protecting their calves from the dog which they see as a threat, but the person with the dog can be trampled to death in such situations, while the dog easily runs away to safety. So, if you feel you need to be in the field, stick to the edges so that you can easily get through or over the fence and thus remain safe. In the minds of cattle, dogs can be a real threat to calves. In America, for instance, coyotes will prey on calves and they have even been known to attack adult cattle if hungry enough. Coyotes are simply wild dogs, so the instinct of cattle to see off dogs which come too near is only natural. Even if there are no calves in a field, still do not go in unless you and your dog can exit very quickly and safely.

Gary Hayes of the Eskdale & Ennerdale Foxhounds with his working Patterdale terrier

If you ever do get into a position where you find yourself in the middle of a field with a herd of large cattle coming at you, then loose the dog and get out of their way. They will simply chase the dog as they are not interested in humans (excepting bulls, which can be dangerous towards humans, so keep out of fields housing bulls). Your dog will easily get away. Just concentrate on your own safety without panicking. Before carrying out livestock training it is best to have your youngster coming to you on command and obeying simple and basic instructions such as the sit, lie-down and stay commands.

When walking near livestock with your trainee secured on a suitably strong lead, jerk the lead and command your puppy to 'leave' in a firm voice which leaves no room for disobedience. Be diligent in keeping such training regular and consistent, but again make certain the sessions are short, with praise and fun games aplenty at the end of each session. This method should be employed with all kinds of livestock, including cats you come across on the street, sheep, cattle, horses, chickens, ducks, geese, or even more exotic animals you may encounter on farms these days such as lamas. Some youngsters will learn almost immediately, while others take time and gradually lose interest in chasing other animals they come across at exercise. For these, more stringent methods can be used in order to instil the lesson more quickly and more firmly.

Carry a thin leather lead in your other hand and as soon as your pet shows any interest in livestock of any kind, crack the lead on the ground in front of it. This acts to distract the thoughts and works well. Use the firm 'leave' command while doing this, together with a strong jerk of the lead attached to the trainee, and the lesson is instilled yet further. Again, regular and consistent sessions are essential. You must be firm in training to leave livestock alone, transmitting to the young trainee that you will not tolerate such behaviour. It may take time, but your pet will eventually learn the lesson and then you can enjoy relaxed walks in the countryside in the full knowledge that your dog will not chase sheep, cattle, horses etc. Such training is vital, but what if, after all your efforts, the youngster weakens and chases livestock?

The first thing to do is not to panic, but to become that figure of authority who has been carrying out training for the past few weeks or months. A firm command of 'leave' repeated several times may stop the offender in its tracks, but if not try the 'stay' command, as this alternative can work. Whilst doing this get yourself into a position, if possible, where you can get between the dog and the sheep, or whatever animal it is chasing, and then crack the lead on the ground several times in front of the dog while firmly commanding it to 'leave.' This should work. Once you have your dog safely secured on a lead, show it in no uncertain terms that it is in your bad books for at least the next few minutes. Never give praise or any kind of treat after such an offence, as it will believe it is being rewarded for its efforts. Livestock training should then continue for a time, until you feel your dog has learnt its lesson. Even if your trainee seems well and truly trustworthy with livestock, provide a refresher course at least once a year throughout its lifetime, just to make certain. Trained dogs can occasionally weaken if the lesson isn't repeated, but reminders will avoid any future problems.

Livestock breaking is essential for all owners of game terriers, but most of all it is essential for those who work their terriers in the countryside and mostly on farmland where livestock graze. Having your terrier chase livestock is the surest way of losing permission to hunt over land and the terrier itself might also be shot and thus lost forever. It is important that those who work terriers are diligent in breaking to livestock, as farmers will simply not tolerate the irresponsible on their land. It does take time and effort to train a dog to leave livestock alone, but the peace of mind one can enjoy while in the countryside makes that effort more than worthwhile.

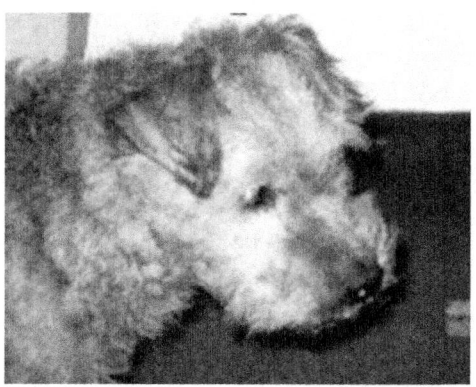

Beck was easy to break to livestock

19. TIPS ON STARTING NOVICE TERRIERS

Many and varied have been the methods of entering Patterdale terriers to more traditional quarry such as the fox and the older hunting folk of the fells employed methods which best suited them. When the more-fiery Lakeland terrier began to breed true to type during the latter part of the nineteenth century it was found that these matured very quickly and most were literally begging for work by the age of nine months, and so several breeders did begin working their charges to large quarry at such a young age. Patterdale terriers are part-bred from those early registered Lakeland terriers, but even so I would not recommend entering to large quarry at such an age. A nine month old terrier is not generally mature enough for tackling large quarry.

Two Reasons for Not Entering too Early

Most fell hunting folk waited and entered their charges later, very often waiting until a terrier was eighteen months of age before putting it to more traditional quarry. This was for two reasons; firstly, because the terriers were not mentally mature enough to cope with a hard-fighting fox, or worse still an incredibly tough badger or fast-striking otter. Early encounters ruined terriers not ready for such large quarry, putting many off earth work for life or making them too hard, which often resulted in them lacking the sense to stay out of trouble and avoid bad maulings, the resultant wounds sometimes being fatal. And, secondly, muscles, bones and teeth are not fully developed until the age of eighteen months and so the more discerning breeders held young terriers back until both fully developed and mentally mature. This ensured that such young entries would take to their work very naturally and that they would be able to cope both mentally and physically with the rough-and-tumble life of a northern working terrier.

George Henry Long of Egremont was one who favoured Lakeland terriers and he felt that any Lakeland was ready for earth work at fox by the age of nine months. His father, a Lake District character called Peter Long, entered his stock at such an age and so he passed this method onto his son. Willie Irving was another who began using some of his terriers at fox by the age of nine months and he learned much of his trade from Willie Porter at the Eskdale and Ennerdale Foxhounds, so these methods were passed on to the next generation. Many, though, as already stated, held their charges back until they reached full maturity at eighteen months and this was undoubtedly the most sensible method.

Some terriers are so keen they need holding back
(Photo courtesy of Tony Swift)

Some also hunted rats and rabbits and entering to such quarry was usually started at around five or six months. Rabbits would be the first quarry and then rats, the terriers being a little older when entering to rats, which could bite hard and put youngsters off. George Henry Long entered to rat at just six months, but most held them back until around eight months or so. Polecats and pinemartens were also hunted until the mid-1900s and terriers would not be entered to these until seven months at least, probably a little later. These creatures, known in Lakeland as 'foumarts' and 'sweetmarts' respectively, struck fast and bit hard, hanging on with jaws like steel traps, so terriers were generally a little on the older side when first starting at such quarry.

'Sandy's' Entering Methods

There is an interesting account regarding the entering of a terrier worked by William Sanderson of Carlisle, whom we discussed earlier in the book. 'Sandy' had many terriers while hunting the Carlisle and District Otterhounds, which were originally kennelled in the city itself. Sanderson entered his stock to marts at around seven months of age and once they had taken to hunting and killing this quarry, gaining some experience, they were entered to otter.

He was patient with his terriers and didn't give up on them if they took some time to catch on, which is a commendable attitude and one which is best employed when entering terriers. It is fair to say that most Patterdale terriers are begging for work by the age of twelve months or so, but it is also true that some, even some of those bred by Breay himself, were slower to start and these must be given time.

The Rewards of Being Patient

John Finney, a sporting farm-worker, always tried to hold back his terriers, even if they were begging for work. He learnt his lesson when he was a young lad, putting a terrier bitch to ground when she was just eight months of age. She encountered a badger and took a bit of a mauling for her troubles. From then on she was far too hard and lacking sense when at large quarry, so after that Finney chose to make certain he kept his youngsters out of earths until they were fourteen or fifteen months of age, though he allowed them to run unoccupied earths before this. He also didn't mind if his terriers wouldn't do much, if anything, during their first spell at large quarry.

He has known his terriers go to a fox, bark at it a few times and return, during a first encounter, but this has not worried him in any way. He simply tried the youngster again the next time and usually, nine times out of ten, the youngster would show much more interest on this occasion, very often staying until dug out, or the quarry decided to bolt. By the third stint to ground his young entry was usually finding unaided and either bolting or staying with their fox as long as necessary. Very few of his terriers needed more than two or three stints at large quarry before they at last caught on and settled to their work, though many of these had been used to flush foxes from dense undergrowth long before going to ground.

John occasionally ratted with his terriers, if any farmer needed some shifting from their yards, but he never put a terrier to rat that he didn't feel was ready to go. Seven or eight months suited his terriers when entering to rat, though some were older, as the occasions he ratted were quite infrequent. Very often his terriers had already seen fox before being entered to rat. He agrees that rats can bite hard, but he has never known a terrier of his to be put off working them after being bitten. One of his bitches once worked several dozen at one session and she never even came close to 'jibbing' (refusing to kill a rat because of previous bites). He considers rats to be small-fry, though he does state that good ratters usually go on to make good fox dogs, in his experience.

Entering Patterdale terriers to quarry is a matter for personal decision, though in my experience the more experienced terrier enthusiasts tend to have more patience. Not only are they willing to wait until their terrier is mature enough for work, but they are willing to wait until it catches on and enters properly. There are no rules in this regard, as some take longer than others. Some seem to be made workers from day one, while others need several stints to ground before finally settling properly. Patience in this regard really is a virtue. Give a dog a chance. Give it time, if you will be working your young terrier. Never force things either. Gentle words of encouragement are enough. And remember to work terriers according to the laws of the country in which you live.

Finney tells a story of a terrier named Grip which well illustrates the importance of being patient and of allowing the terrier to develop at its own pace. Grip was put into a crag earth, in a cleft between the rocks, where the fox was skulking on a ledge a few feet inside. Grip went in and had a good sniff around, bayed a few times and then emerged, uninterested in further proceedings. The next time he was put to ground he went like a Trojan, charging at his fox and driving it to the end of the drain where Finney was able to pull it out, or, rather, where his hound, Merlin, pulled it out. So never write off a terrier which at first shows little interest in work.

One terrierman who worked his charges with a northern pack of hounds tells a tale of one of his terriers which wouldn't enter to fox no matter what he tried. He was almost at the end of his tether when one day hounds roused a fox, which ran to ground in a crag earth after giving hounds a good hunt across the face of the wide sweeping moors. Risking much embarrassment, he decided to give his bitch one last try and surprisingly she entered the earth eagerly, disappearing into the dark recesses of the rocks, finding her fox, baying at it and then finally bolting it. She never looked back after that and the terrierman was glad that he had given his bitch time to settle to her work.

This experience also well illustrates the need to be patient with a young terrier, which needs time to mature in order to settle to its work properly. A terrier may not even look at an earth for months and then one day it disappears to ground and works like a Trojan. Some will go to ground and bolt foxes, but refuse to stay if they will not bolt. John Finney tells a tale of one of his bitches, Myrt, which was like this. One day though, she went to ground, bolted a large dog fox after a fierce tussle and then found and killed a vixen in the same earth. Finney had to dig her out and he told of his delight when his bitch finally entered properly.

Gryke was of a similar disposition. This was yet another of Finney's terriers which was bred out of much Border terrier stock, being descended from Buck/Breay/Akerigg breeding. He was a powerfully built terrier and Finney looked forward to entering him to quarry. He tried this dog at around fourteen months of age, to a fox in a drain that had been marked-in by hounds. Rush was baying eagerly at the fox, but it would not bolt. Finney thought it the ideal time to try Gryke, so he loosed the dog, expecting him to enter very well indeed, but, though Gryke went right up to the fox and had a little bark at it, he very quickly emerged.

Finney left him loose while Rush continued to attempt to bolt it, hoping the dog would enter, but he just went in and out of the earth a few times, until Finney decided to dig out Rush and her fox. The drain was around four or five feet deep and the dig was difficult, but Gryke never entered properly to that fox. The very next outing saw a fox marked to ground in a moorland earth, a dug-out rabbit hole on the edge of the moor, and Gryke was put in. This time he worked a little more seriously, but emerged about twenty minutes later. The fox wasn't going to bolt, so Finney decided to move off and draw for another, but Gryke, still loose, suddenly ran back to the earth, disappeared below ground and failed to emerge. John eventually dug-out his terrier, which had finished his fox, a big dog fox, inside the earth. Imagine if Finney had written off the terrier after his lack of interest during that first stint to earth and had got rid of him, as some do. A great terrier would have been lost, as Gryke went on to become one of the best terriers Finney has ever seen at work, and he has seen lots of terriers working to fox over the years. So be patient when entering and give a terrier a chance!

The Batty family with what I am certain are Breay-bred terriers, after a successful day in 1936

Breay's entering methods

Although much about Cyril Breay remains a mystery, one thing known about him is that he never put a terrier to large quarry before the age of twelve months, or a little after. We also know that Breay was very careful when entering youngsters, showing much patience and never speaking to them in anything other than his usual voice. He would also usually work a young entry alongside a more experienced terrier at first, of which he usually had several to choose from. Breay bred some very excitable terriers during his later years and Bingo and Rusty were two of these, so it is unlikely that such stock, which were hysterically keen to latch onto their quarry (yet another indication of bull terrier blood having some influence on later breeding, particularly from the late 1940s or early 1950s), would have been suited to working below ground alongside another terrier. Breay's patience, as well as that of Frank Buck who was also an expert at entering terriers (though Frank Buck learnt much of his trade from Cyril Breay), is worth emulating when starting a novice working terrier. Being patient, calm and kind *always* works when entering the right sort of terrier.

20. TIPS ON SHOWING TERRIERS

Showing terriers can be enjoyable and classes for Patterdale, or black fell terriers are very often put on at working terrier shows and game fairs, with many hunts up and down the country also staging fundraising shows where terrier classes are included. 'Crossbred' classes are put on at some shows and Patterdale terriers are very often entered in crossbred classes. Classes for Patterdale terriers should be separate however. There are now plenty of Patterdale terriers after this type has greatly increased in popularity, so it is about time that all shows catered for this type of terrier.

The Correct Class

Crossbred classes are not exactly labelled properly, as many Patterdale terriers are bred as carefully as pedigree terriers and should now be considered as a breed in their own right, or at least as a distinct type of fell terrier, so separate classes should be put on for them, even though it is true to say that the Patterdale was developed from the same rootstock as Border and Lakeland terriers. If, however, there are no classes for Patterdale terriers, then use either the fell class or the crossbred class, as most Patterdale terriers will not compete against the sharper lines of the Lakeland terrier. Some do favour black Lakeland terriers however, and these could be entered in Lakeland classes, but it is always best to have separate classes for Patterdale terriers.

The author judging at Patterdale

It is best not to take exhibiting too seriously, though it is also good to put in some effort to at least compete, giving your terrier a good shot at winning, or at least picking up a rosette. Shows really took off in the Lake District during the 1860s after the first dog show staged in 1859 in Newcastle started a craze which eventually had a massive impact on type. Those early shows were staged in conjunction with agricultural shows throughout the Lakes, though some became more prestigious than others and serious terrier breeding in order to improve type began to spread throughout the country, not just the region, during the latter half of the nineteenth century and well into the twentieth. Grasmere Sports, Rydal Hound Show (terrier section) and Keswick show, and those staged in and around Egremont, were some of the most prestigious and influential of the Lakeland terrier shows and any serious breeder wanted to win these events. It is good to have some ambition with regard to showing, but it is best to have a more light-hearted outlook, as disappointment will often be experienced regularly at this game.

Improving Type
The old fell type, then known mostly as coloured working terriers, fell, or fellside terriers, was bred for work and so type was nothing special, with many terriers being of poor quality from an aesthetic point of view, so breeders set out to improve conformation and some smart terriers were already being produced as early as the late 1860s. Robinson of Egremont and Peter Long were two of the most successful early breeders of what later became known as the Lakeland terrier and Robinson actually made part of his living by breeding and selling typey terriers capable of winning at shows, despite some classes in those days having as many as a hundred or more entries in each class. Robinson and Peter Long had a massive influence on terrier breeding during the late 1800s and early 1900s, as did the Kitchen family of Ennerdale and Egremont. Jim Dalton's terriers were also extremely typey and the Blencathra Foxhounds' Huntsman bred Blencathra Turk during the first decade of the twentieth century. Turk was used by Peter Long to mate his bitches, as well as many other keen breeders such as Chris 'Kitty' Farrer at the Ullswater.

Type varied greatly in those days, with some terriers displaying much Bedlington about them, while others, such as the old Patterdale type which, incidentally, was bred throughout the Lakes, not just in Patterdale, resembled workmanlike Border terriers, but with better coats. As early as the 1860s staff at the Melbreak Foxhounds bred and worked what were described by their Master, Squire John Benson, as "reddish, strong-haired and courageous" terriers and these may well have been early Patterdale terriers. As we have seen, modern Patterdale terriers were partly bred from

Border terriers, the old original type kept by Frank Buck and Cyril Breay being a mixture of old fell bloodlines, Sealyham terrier bloodlines and Border terrier blood from the Bedale, Zetland and Lunesdale Hunts in particular. It is also true to say that Lakeland terrier blood also played a part and Breay and Buck greatly improved type in their terriers during the 1940s when they introduced such blood via Tear 'Em and a son of Tear 'Em. Later, Harry Hardisty's famous Turk was used as outcross blood as Breay believed that Harry Hardisty was the best terrier breeder in the north and that his Turk was an outstanding looker and worker, which, of course, was true. Turk greatly improved type and he in turn was bred down from Willie Irving's famous strain of working registered Lakeland terrier.

Preparing for a Show

One of the keys to success when exhibiting terriers is to make the effort to prepare properly. Terrier shows where Patterdale terriers can be exhibited are not for the typical pampered pet which has been groomed until its hair is silky and soft, and adorned with pink ribbons, but still, some effort needs to be put in before a show.

I would not recommend bathing just before a show. A judge worth his salt will be concerned with, not only coat type, but he will also be looking for weatherproofing within that coat. A breed of working terrier should have an oily jacket as this will repel rainwater and thus protect the wearer from the elements. Bathing will reduce oiliness for some time afterwards, so this is best avoided, or carried out a few days before a show. A good judge will rub the hair between fingers and thumb in order to ascertain the oiliness of a terrier's jacket. He (or she, of course!) will also be looking for tightness and denseness in a coat. This again helps repel rainwater and keeps cold winds at bay.

A cold and sodden terrier would be at risk of dying of exposure when rainwater and icy winds get at the skin, so a decent jacket is vital. Patterdale terriers often have rough coats and these can be greatly improved by stripping-out the jacket just before the show season begins, most of which are staged in spring, summer and early autumn. Many, of course, come with smooth or slightly broken coats which need little attention, apart from a regular grooming. Grooming spreads the natural oils and improves the look of a jacket, so should be carried out before exhibiting.

A stripping knife can be purchased from any decent pet store, or on Amazon or Ebay, or some other internet site, at reasonable cost and this is used to pull out the longer hairs which can look unsightly. Always remember to do this with the growth of hair, not against it, just as a carpenter works along with the grain, not against it. Pulling out the longer hairs will neaten and tighten the coat and will encourage new growth; hard and wiry new growth, which will appear within a very short time, when your terrier will at last be ready for exhibiting. Strip-out the long hair on the legs and paws too. Little stripping is usually needed around the head and face, though some stripping to tidy-up appearance will be necessary. Avoid using scissors where possible as cutting the jacket will only ruin the wiry texture and spoil the colour.

Stripping-out the jacket is the main task of preparation, though it is also beneficial to make certain that the eyes are clean and that the terrier is neither too fat, nor too thin. A light grooming just before the show is beneficial, as is making certain that the dog generally is clean and of neat appearance. Never exhibit a terrier with unhealed bites as this creates a very bad impression and gives terrier-work a bad name. Scars from treated and healed bites, on the other hand, are nothing to be ashamed of as they are inevitable when terriers are worked at any biting quarry, even rats. Breay's terriers were battle-scarred, as were Frank Buck's. At one show a battle-scarred terrier was being exhibited and a kennel club judge, who had no right judging a working terrier class, asked what they were. "Those" replied Cyril Breay indignantly, "are medals!!!"

There is now nothing more one can do, as judges will have individual tastes and will make up their own minds as to which of the exhibits will be given prizes, and in what order, though it is good to have an idea of what judges will be looking for in the show-ring. Do not forget, these are working terrier shows, so points which suit work will be considered when judging.

General Type & Spanning
The first thing a judge will look for is general type; a workmanlike appearance so as to ascertain that the terrier is not too big for the

job or that it is not too long in the body, or indeed, too short in the body so as to hamper free movement. A terrier which is too long in the body will suffer back problems when working tight earths. One that is too short in the body may really struggle to negotiate tight and narrow places. So free movement and correct size, are essential qualities. Checking that a terrier is spannable is also vital at working terrier shows.

spannable and workmanlike
(Photo courtesy of Tony Swift)

This is done by placing one's hands directly behind the shoulders of the terrier and enclosing them around the back and ribs. If thumbs meet at the top and fingers meet below the chest, then a terrier is spannable and can get into most earths. However, commonsense should prevail when spanning. If a judge has very small hands, for instance, then he could not expect his fingers to meet below the ribs. He must then judge the distance between and discern what is, and what is not, acceptable. If a judge has huge hands and a dog is only-just spannable, then it is likely too big in the chest. Each judge must use discernment when using such fallible methods.

Leg Length & General Size

Length of leg is less important than the spannability of a terrier required to work in what are often narrow earths. This is because a terrier can fold its legs under its body, or stretch them out behind. As long as a terrier is narrow enough in the chest to get below ground, then length of leg is far less of an issue. Again, discernment must be exercised when judging and experience will usually aid a judge in making correct decisions. A loose guide would be that a terrier above fifteen inches at the shoulder would usually struggle badly to get in most earths, though there are always exceptions to rules.

Dick Peel, Honorary Master and lifelong supporter of the Blencathra Foxhounds, tells tales of a famous terrier called Red Ike which worked with the 'Cathra during the 1930s (from 1933 to 1937 to be precise) and ran loose with hounds. Ike was a large terrier, sixteen inches in height, yet he could work out foxes from most places in the fells, such as deep borrans and the infamous peat earths found particularly in the Caldbeck Fells district. Ike, in fact, was a grand terrier to work, despite his large size, so a terrier should not be 'knocked' by a judge unless it is above fifteen or sixteen inches at the shoulder (spannability and other points will be considered in such situations, with decisions being based on experience too).

Can a terrier be too small? Some very small terriers have worked with the fell packs, so it is difficult to say, but a terrier with very short legs would surely struggle to cover rough country and jump on and off ledges below ground. A terrier with short legs will never match type in taller terriers anyway, so exhibiting such stock may be a fruitless pursuit. Again, discernment in making judgements is the general rule. Do not forget, though, that Cyril Breay stopped using Sealyham terriers because they were too short legged for the rough fells he began hunting. One thing I do like to see on a terrier are straight legs, though I will not 'knock' one with feet that turn-out slightly, as long as its movement is free and natural. Straight legs adorn foxes and they are incredibly agile. Straight legs have also aided terriers working narrow crag ledges in order to flush foxes 'binking' there. Showing your terrier can be great fun, as can be entering them in terrier races. Some shows include racing, while many do not, but have a go, as this can be both entertaining and rewarding. My best result was with Ghyll when he was reserve champion in the terrier racing at Langdale many years ago. He was beaten to the championship by an incredibly fast and agile Jack Russell with very short legs! One thing to remember when staging terrier racing; make certain that people are ready at the finishing line to quickly grab their dogs, in order to prevent major dog fights which may result in serious injury or even death if not stopped quickly. Especially if a terrier catches the lure, can fights break out, so be quick to get hold of your dog at the finish of a race.

A grand sort for work or show

21. TIPS ON BREEDING

I have a policy of never breeding for monetary gain (though there is little money in terrier breeding anyway) and only breed a litter when I need a youngster or two to replace ageing terriers. I believe there are enough unwanted dogs on the planet and so do not wish to contribute in any way to this trend. I also believe there are a number of excellent breeders out there and sometimes I do not breed at all, but purchase stock from others instead. This, of course, is a personal decision and it is up to each owner of Patterdale terriers to decide what they will do.

Some say that a bitch must have at least one litter during its lifetime in order to ensure good health, but I have found this to be untrue. A bitch will be fine if not mated, so do not feel pressured to breed if that is not what you wish to do. If you do decide to breed, then do so responsibly. I have had no serious health problems with any of my bitches which have not been used for breeding a litter. In fact, at the time of writing Beck is thirteen years of age and is still going strong.

If I wish to replace ageing or dead stock, then I do my utmost to find potential homes for at least one or two puppies *before* breeding a litter, while at the same time making it clear that the bitch may fail to conceive, or only have one or two puppies which the breeder may wish to keep. Avoid making guarantees when seeking potential homes for puppies, just in case things do not work out. This is not always possible I know, but even if you can find homes for just one or two puppies besides those you will keep for yourself, it is at least something.

Advertising in local papers or publications which deal specifically with this breed, such as *The Countryman's Weekly*, or similar publications distributed around the country in which you live, will no doubt succeed in finding homes for any surplus stock, but, of course, advertisements are best placed when the puppies are nearing eight weeks of age, which is the minimum age for a puppy to leave its dam. Facebook pages or other internet sites dealing with terrier sales may also prove fruitful places for advertising, but be careful to avoid any who do not seem like decent breeders.

The Brood Bitch & the Stud Dog

The main quality of both potential breeding terriers is a good temperament. I would not advise anyone to breed from a terrier, dog or bitch that is aggressive with other dogs and especially with children. Only terriers which are sound family dogs should be bred from. The ancestors of modern Patterdale terriers were often kennelled with hounds and were worked alongside other terriers, so aggression was not tolerated and aggressive dogs and bitches were often not bred from. This ensured mostly excellent temperaments, which makes this breed so appealing. Thus future breeders should aim to produce youngsters with equally good temperaments. Usually two terriers of good temperament will produce offspring with similar qualities.

Another priority should be to make certain that both the brood bitch and the stud dog are healthy and constitutionally sound, with neither having any serious faults. Good coat on both potential parents is also a priority, more especially if you will either be working or showing your terrier, or perhaps both. A poor coat will not endear your terrier to any judge of a working terrier show. If your terrier will simply be a family pet, then coat may not be important to you, but it will likely be important to potential buyers. So good coat should be essential for both the dog and bitch terrier. Avoid using a terrier with a soft and silky open coat. The jacket on a Patterdale terrier should either be smooth (slape-coated in Lake District terminology), or rough and wiry, not soft and silky. A coat should not be sparse either, but dense enough to keep out the cold and wet.

Neither the dog nor the bitch should have poor mouths, either undershot or overshot. The teeth should meet in a strong scissor-bite. The ears should not be too large and they should be drop-ears, not pricked-up like those of a Scottish terrier, though there will always be a small percentage of Patterdale terriers which continue to produce this prick-ear in litters, so being realistic one can do little to stop this from cropping up in some puppies.

Size is an issue, as this breed should not exceed fifteen inches at the shoulder, though around thirteen or fourteen inches is a more desirable size. It is difficult to guarantee size in the offspring of a dog and bitch, but generally speaking if a dog and bitch are not too big, then most, if not all, of the offspring should not be too big.

A good sort to breed from

Can a stud dog or brood bitch be too small? If the legs are too short for the owner to cross rough country, then the answer has to be, yes. A Patterdale terrier must have enough leg length to cross rough hill country at a decent pace – at least that of a fast walking man or woman. If a terrier has to be picked up and carried across rough country, then it is too small. I have visited many of the places hunted by both Breay and Buck and I can assure you that a short-legged terrier would find it impossible to cover much of this ground. Do not forget, Breay forsook short-legged Sealyham terriers because they were not suited to hunting fell country.

The Stud Fee
Having found a suitable stud dog, one can expect to pay anything from fifty pounds to the price of a puppy as the fee, or the owner will ask for 'pick of the litter' as his fee instead, which is quite reasonable. Giving the owner of the stud dog first choice is usual practise, so it is best not to choose which you will be keeping until

after the stud fee puppy has been chosen. If conception fails, then any breeder worth his salt will offer the free services of his stud dog when the bitch next comes in season.

Finding a stud dog is not always easy, but this can be done by scanning through advertisements and especially by attending terrier shows and getting familiar with some of the breeders who exhibit their charges.

The Mating

The bitch will come into season and the best time for the mating to occur is the twelfth, thirteenth and fourteenth days after bleeding begins. Your bitch will be most fertile at this time. The bitch can be taken to the dog for servicing, though a successful mating will occur if the dog is taken to the bitch too. This is a matter for convenience and personal choice, but make certain, wherever the mating is to occur, that there are no other dogs or bitches anywhere near the breeding pair. Also, a small space is far better than a large one, as a stud dog and brood bitch can be worn out by running around a large enclosed area.

Create a relaxed atmosphere as best you can. Supervise the mating, but be quiet and relaxed about doing so, as dogs will pick up on nervous or excitable vibes. Other than that, leave them to it. They will usually manage quite alright by themselves, though sometimes a mating will fail to occur. My own dog Turk was put to a Bedlington bitch and she just wouldn't accept him, no matter what he tried. One can do nothing but shrug one's shoulders and accept it if a mating fails. You can assist by holding the bitch for the stud dog or even by trying to guide him in, should he be struggling, but even then some attempts to mate do fail.

A dog and bitch will tie, but the length of time a tie lasts for will vary. Sometimes they will tie for just a few minutes, at other times for twenty minutes or even longer. This time can be boring, so have a cup of tea, while keeping a close eye on the tied pair. A tie is vital for conception, so do not try to rush them. They will part naturally in their own time. It may be necessary to assist the dog, helping him to get his leg over (no pun intended) the bitch so that they are back to back. This is the most comfortable position when a tie occurs. If the bitch is over-excitable and continually tries to pull away during a tie, then it is best to hold her in order to make things more comfortable for the dog terrier.

Phil Brogden's Britt – a looker & worker

The dog will look abnormal when they do part, but the penis will soon withdraw back into the sheath after a short duration and he will be back to himself in no time at all, though he will usually be a little more pleased with himself than he was before meeting his intended! Two matings are enough, though one should also prove to be enough if a second mating is inconvenient or even impossible due to circumstances. The second mating can be done on the same day if that is convenient, after the pair has rested for a few hours, though it is best to wait until the next day for the second mating. Make a note of the date of both matings, for nine weeks later a litter of puppies will likely be born, if all has gone well. This could be nine weeks after the first mating, or nine weeks after the second, depending on when conception occurred.

Care of the Pregnant Bitch
General opinion is that a bitch should not be mated until she is at

least twelve months of age, but I would not advise breeding from a bitch until she is at least two years old, as by this time she will be both physically and mentally mature enough to cope with the demands made upon her. A bitch should also be wormed using a multi-wormer preferably from the vet before she comes in season. She should also have fleas removed from her skin and bedding. When worming and getting rid of fleas always follow the instructions provided.

The bitch should be fed normally for the first four weeks of pregnancy and then one extra meal should be added. I usually feed cereal such as weetabix, with a little glucose and watered-down milk added, in a morning, with her usual meal given in the evening. This should suffice, though portions can be increased if necessary. Make certain that fresh water is always available and if giving extra drinks of milk it is best to water it down a little and take the chill out of it, serving it at room temperature or even a little warmer, not straight out of the fridge. Do not give too much milk, as this will likely be too rich and will upset her stomach. If you wish to use supplements, then talk to your vet and get the right advice before doing so.

In the seventh week get your bitch settled in her whelping box, which can be wooden, or made of very sturdy cardboard. The bitch should have easy access, but you will want to keep the puppies confined once they begin walking and running around. Thus the sides of the box should be high enough to restrict the puppies, yet low enough to allow the bitch to get in and out easily. The sides must also be low enough to allow the bitch to see her pups, so that she doesn't jump on any of them when getting in.

This box should be roomy enough for bitch and growing puppies and should be placed in a dry, warm, but not hot, place; out of direct sunlight and far enough away from heaters to avoid discomfort to the occupants. The bedding can be old newspapers or shredded paper, which I find is the best material to use. This is easily disposed of and the whelping box is thus easily kept clean and infection free. Remember to inform your vet in good time of the date your bitch is due to whelp, considering that the second mating may have been the one which resulted in conception, just in case of any emergencies. Patterdale terriers suffer few problems when whelping, but occasionally things can go wrong and an emergency call to the vet may be necessary. This is just a precaution and will likely not be necessary.

The Birth

Your bitch will become unsettled when labour sets in and will likely scratch around in her bed. Labour can last a good few hours, so be as relaxed as possible. Your bitch will sense anxieties and tension, so help her to be as settled as possible by keeping calm and relaxed (not easy, I know!). As the birth nears the pregnant bitch may vomit, but do not worry, this is quite normal. It is best to supervise the birth if at all possible, though you may wake up in the morning and all is well with the new family.

My bitch Mist gave me no choice in the matter, as she went into hysterics the night she was due, when I tried going to bed. I was forced to stay up with her and slept on the couch, as she screamed like a banshee when I attempted to leave her. She gave birth to six healthy puppies during the early hours and on the next night she again went into hysterics as I tried to go to bed, as though she was telling me not to leave her alone "with this lot!" That was her first litter and she took time to settle with them, but after that first night she was fine and proved to be an excellent mother. Keep a close eye on the bitch and if there are any complications it may be best to telephone for the vet. If the bitch fails to bite the cord, thus freeing the puppy from the afterbirth, then cut it yourself with a pair of sterilized blunt scissors, making the cut well away from the body.

The Growing Litter & Tail-Docking

After the birth is over, which may take a few hours, allow your bitch out into the garden, if she will leave her litter that is, while you clean out the whelping box. From then on clean it out regularly, for the paper will become badly soiled. Your bitch will take care of the puppies, while you take care of the bitch, giving her ample food and drink. At three days of age tail-docking can be carried out, but this is best done by a qualified vet, if laws in the country in which you live allow for this.

Is docking necessary? In some cases, yes, especially if the terrier will be worked, as tails are notoriously bad healers and if damaged can sometimes fail to heal and amputation is then the only answer. The problem is, with adult dogs amputation can also result in a failure of the wound to heal and a dog will then have to be put down. Docking at three to five days of age is far better. A quick snip and it is done, with little fuss. The puppies settle almost immediately after and healing is usually very quick. Docking is not cruel, but necessary in some instances, though I do believe that docking just for exhibiting purposes is unnecessary. Also, there is a case for docking when it comes to terriers going to ground. It would be a very rare occurrence, but a long tail could become lodged in tree roots or between a cleft in rocks, which would result in the terrier becoming trapped. So docking working terriers is, I believe, essential. My own vet agreed and he was happy to dock my puppies.

Worming can be carried out from about three weeks of age using products from the vet or pet store, but make certain you carefully follow the directions. Also watch out for the symptoms of milk fever, though this condition is rare. Restlessness, rapid breathing and convulsions, or fits, may signal this condition, so call out the vet immediately. This is a life threatening illness and must be treated as quickly as possible.

Stroke and handle the puppies as soon as the dam will allow this without being disturbed or upset in any way, and allow your children to carefully and gently handle them too, as this will greatly aid the socialising process (always make certain the bitch is happy for you and your children to handle her puppies). The eyes will begin opening at between two and three weeks of age and at around three weeks the pups will be beginning to take tentative steps around the whelping box. You will soon come to appreciate why those sides need to be high enough to keep pups in, but allow them out for play and exercise once they are steady on their feet.

Weaning

I usually wean puppies at around four weeks of age, though this can be done sooner if the bitch isn't giving them enough milk, or she is drying up (a restless litter will signal a problem with milk supplies). Softened cereal with warm milk is best for the first few days and then softened puppy food will suffice, such as a complete meal puppy food. At around eight to ten weeks they should not need the puppy food softened anymore, but should be able to tackle it dry, unless the instructions on the packet advise softening until a later age. Again, follow instructions carefully.

It is best to dock the tails of working Patterdale terriers, as injured tails are notoriously bad at healing

Provide a drink of watered-down milk slightly warmed after each meal, but do not put a bowl of water in the whelping box with them, for obvious reasons. It will just be spilled all over the place, or will be badly soiled in no time. Never have deep bowls of water in a puppy's environment, or buckets of water for that matter, as they can fall in and drown. Like having children, think about their environment and of how you can make it as safe as possible. Exercise and play periods should also be closely supervised.

Continue to provide the bitch with extra food, but as the puppies eat more solid food provided for them after weaning, you can begin to cut down on that given to the mother. Use commonsense, if your bitch looks too thin, then feed her up. If she is becoming obese, then cut her food down. She will need less as the puppies reach eight weeks of age, when it is time to sell them on to their new owners. Do your utmost to make certain they go to good homes and one way to do this is not to sell them too cheaply. Ask a good price for them. At the time of writing a well bred Patterdale puppy will fetch about £150.00-£200.00, or even more if they are show winning parents. An idiot is less likely to pay good money for a puppy, so do not "give" them away by asking little money for your litter.

The only other advice I can give is to be diligent about keeping the whelping box clean. The bitch will clean after her puppies soil, but the bedding will still become dirty in a relatively short time, so clean it out regularly, making certain the box is clean when potential buyers come to view the litter. It is best to exercise your puppies out in the garden if the weather allows and if the puppies cannot get under or through the fence, and the garden is safe for them, otherwise try to exercise them on kitchen flooring, which is easily cleaned, as they will create a mess very quickly. If exercising in the garden with a pond in it, then keep a very close eye on your puppies. Only a minute or so lapse in concentration could end in tragedy if a puppy falls into the water.

22. FIRST AID & CARE OF THE ELDERLY TERRIER

First aid in this chapter is about dealing with only minor cuts and injuries, not anything more serious that should be treated by a vet as soon as possible. This includes minor bites from quarry such as rats and foxes. Such creatures can occasionally be encountered by terriers kept as pets, not just as working dogs, so it is good to have in mind a few basics when it comes to first aid.

Treating Minor Injuries
First of all it is good to remember that cuts, bites and scratches need

to be both cleaned and allowed to dry in fresh air, so it is best not to use creams which will only keep the wound moist. A moist wound is more prone to infection, so allowing the wound to dry up as soon as possible is essential to fast healing. In my experience, and I have treated many wounds over the thirty and more years I have now been keeping terriers, there is nothing better than a few dabs of TCP, or something similar, or just plain salt water, for treating minor wounds. Allow the treated area to dry naturally and do not cover with anything at all. Bathing such wounds regularly, maybe as many as four or five times a day, will keep wounds clean and fresh air will do the rest. Anything more serious than minor cuts, scratches and bites should be treated by a vet and bandages may be applied to some more serious injuries.

Checking the eyes after exercising and work periods is essential. Debris such as grass seeds can easily be removed or an eye wash can be applied in order to get rid of anything which may cause harm to the eyes. If you cannot remove such debris yourself, then a visit to the vet may be necessary. Such bits left in the eyes can cause infections, so they are best removed as quickly as possible.

Regular grooming, preferably every day after exercise periods, will help drag out any thorns or other potentially harmful debris from the jacket and checking the paws is another good measure after exercise, especially after periods in the countryside. Thorns stuck in pads can cause major problems if they become deeply embedded, so do your utmost to remove these quickly. If you notice your terrier is lame in one of its feet as you are out walking then it is prudent to check the paws immediately, as thorns are easilypicked up when they stick into the outer tissue of the pad. Basic first aid and preventative measures such as those described may save you quite a bit of money which would otherwise be spent at the local veterinary surgery. Untreated cuts, bites and scratches and debris left in eyes, or thorns in pads can cause infections, which then means having to visit the vet who will likely administer antibiotics, but it is far better to avoid such infections in the first place. It is not cheap visiting your local vet these days, so any way of saving money, as long as the welfare of your terrier is not compromised of course, is more than welcome.

The Elderly Terrier
It is sad to see a terrier slowing down as it reaches old age and one of the first things I have noticed in my ageing dogs is that they tend to get weaker in the back legs. A terrier with weakening back legs should no longer be worked to ground, as it will struggle to jump on and off ledges and agility in tight and narrow spaces may also have deteriorated, though no doubt it will continue to enjoy bushing work, or perhaps a spot of ratting.

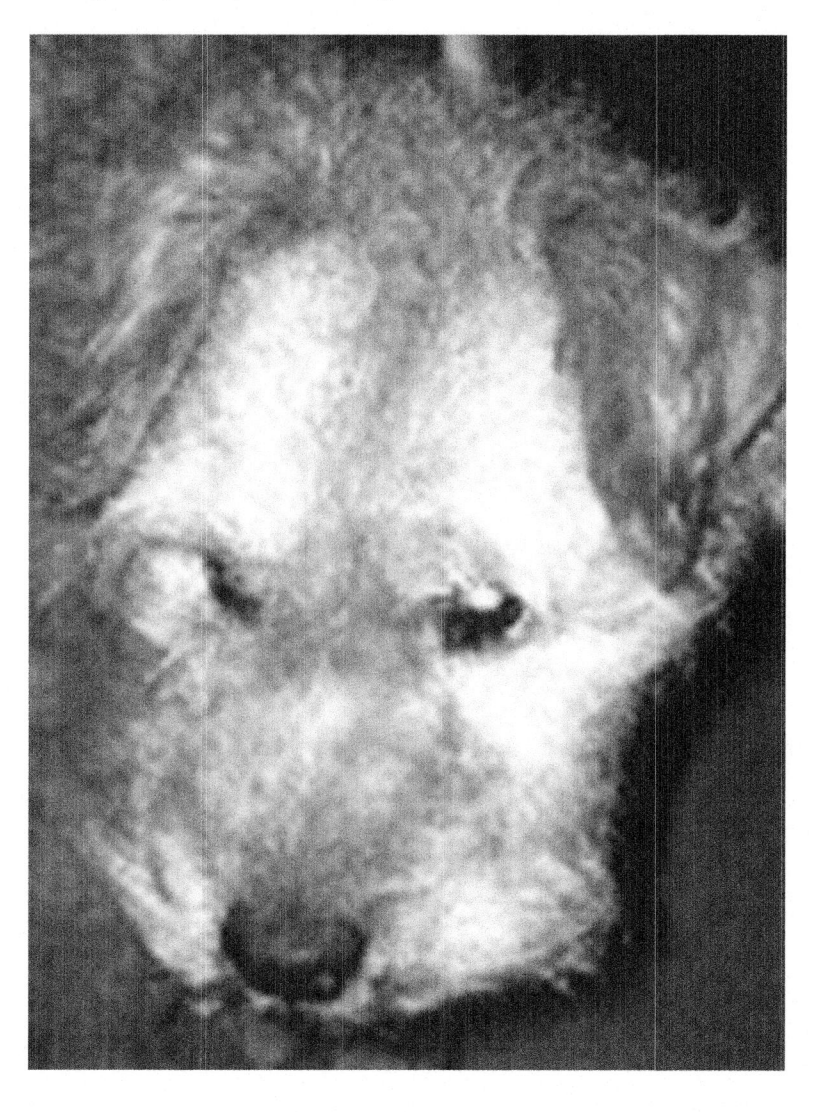

An elderly terrier belonging to the author

The eyes may lighten, but this does not necessarily mean they are going blind. Some of my old terriers have had almost white eyes, yet have shown no signs of blindness. Deafness may gradually increase as a dog gets older, so stop working a terrier that is deaf and be careful at exercise when it is loose, as deaf dogs can easily wander and be lost. Micro-chipping will help recovery, but there is always the chance that a lost dog can wander onto a busy road and be killed, so take great care with the elderly and keep a close eye on them at exercise.

Looked after properly, Patterdale terriers will enjoy good health for years to come

Elderly terriers may begin to need less food, the older they get, so keep an eye on weight, cutting down food if you notice your terrier is becoming obese. Avoid obesity in older dogs especially, as this will only shorten their lifespan. A terrier fed correctly and exercised regularly will hardly ever be at the vet and it will go on to enjoy a long life, giving you much pleasure over a number of years.

When to retire the working Patterdale terrier?

It isn't easy giving exact times as to when a working terrier should be retired, for it mostly depends on how well each individual terrier ages. Also, a terrier could go on bushing or ratting for some time after being retired from earth work. The main reason for retiring from earth work is that a terrier needs to be at its fittest if it is to work foxes out of their lairs. An ageing terrier will decline in both strength and agility as it gets advanced in years, though some fare better than others. Some terriers have worked to ground into their teen years, though I would not recommend this. Breay's Gem was still working at the age of eight or nine years, in spite of her injuries after falling into that ghyll at Barbondale.

In the spring of 1958 Breay was called out by a gamekeeper at Barbondale who had found a litter of cubs at a place known as the 'three little boys' where three mountain becks meet. The earth was a dug-out rabbit hole and was extremely tight, which meant that Gem struggled to get, as did Skiffle. Breay and the keeper persisted, but the cubs managed to stay out of reach generally, though one of the terriers, either Gem or Skiffle, Robin cannot remember exactly which, did account for one of the cubs. So Gem was still active at that age, though she died two years after falling into that Barbondale ghyll while at work with the Lunesdale Foxhounds.

Again, retirement depends on the individual terrier, but if one gets eight seasons out of a working terrier then that is most satisfactory, though some work for longer than this. Terriers generally do not cope well with retirement, as they are keen to work even into old age, so after retiring from earth work it may be a good idea to continue bushing and ratting with them, as this will keep them active and thus happy. Commonsense should prevail and when it becomes obvious that a terrier is not coping very well with work, then retirement should immediately follow. If a terrier is becoming increasingly deaf, then retirement is best, as a deaf terrier can easily lose touch with its master and become lost. Again, use commonsense, as only each individual owner can make the decision to retire a valued working terrier.

Exercise of the Elderly

If you notice that your terrier is struggling with exercise periods and is even reluctant to go out, then you may be walking too far. Shorten the exercise periods in this case and your ageing terrier will no doubt once again find pleasure in its walks. If your dog is persistent in being reluctant to go on walks, even though you have shortened them, then it is simply telling you that it has had enough. In such cases a wander around the garden a few times a day will undoubtedly suffice from then on, until the end of its life (a terrier which is reluctant to go on exercise is usually close to the end of its life). The reward one gets from a good-natured terrier is well worth the effort of diligent care and, as the terrier gets older, kind consideration.

13. THE FUTURE FOR PATTERDALE TERRIERS

I believe that the future for Patterdale terriers is bright and for two reasons. Firstly, the Patterdale remains a superb working terrier that is often too game for its own good. During the 1950s and 1960s Breay and Buck-bred terriers began attacking their quarry at the first opportunity and some would grab hold of their fox anywhere and take fearful punishment, which may well have been a result of bull terrier blood being added at some point. Certainly the line that produced Bingo and Rusty was often hysterically keen to work and both Bingo and Rusty greatly irritated Breay, because they were so hysterically keen to get to ground. Breay would often send his son, Robin, away with Bingo, lest his eagerness disturbed a bolting fox. If a fox wouldn't bolt, then Bingo got his chance and the fox would soon be destroyed once he got to earth. Sense is still lacking in some Patterdale terriers, though it is true to say that many do make good and sensible workers.

It is for such reasons that I would advise against using any more bull terrier blood in Patterdale terrier bloodlines, which simply makes them too hard and also produces large chests which hampers work underground (many of the Patterdale terriers I have judged have been too broad in the chest and have thus been unspannable).

A good strong strain of working border terriers, or even fell terriers, would be far better for use as outcross blood, though only occasional use of such outcross blood should be employed. Any stud dog used as outcross blood should be sensible and game, as well as have good general type and good hard coat.

Secondly, Patterdale terriers usually have sound temperaments which make them ideal as family pets and show dogs. True, some rescued terriers have been damaged through some kind of trauma (sometimes neglect, or even physical abuse), but well socialised terriers from careful selective breeding are usually great with children and are quiet around other dogs.

Terrier shows & racing help secure a bright future for Patterdale terriers

Shows are still popular and many more venues put on classes for Patterdale terriers. They are also quick enough to compete in terrier racing, which is very entertaining. There are Patterdale terrier clubs and several Patterdale terrier groups on facebook, so their popularity continues to grow and many celebrate the massive appeal of this type of working breed of terrier. It is because of this popularity that I can confidently state that Patterdale terriers will continue to prosper, though breeders must be responsible and try to avoid breeding from any dog or bitch with serious faults.

Away they go

Undershot and overshot mouths, a lack of a full set of teeth and good bone structure and poor coats, as well as bad temperaments, are just some faults that are not worth continuing in any bloodline. On the other hand, terriers with few, if any, faults are the ones to breed from, but outcross blood every few generations is essential to prevent the gene pool from shrinking and weaknesses from becoming dominant traits.

In my opinion, the future for the Patterdale terrier should not include Kennel Club recognition, as this will only ruin the type

Breay and Buck bred, as well as modern breeders whose stock is popular today. Breeding for show purposes has ruined many breeds and we do not want such a future for the still-game and characterful Patterdale terrier.

Breay's Tig, Rusty, Bonny & Monty
(1960s)

Cyril Breay with Rusty on Leck Fell

24. A-Z OF PATTERDALE TERRIER NAMES

Adder: A poisonous snake found in the British Isles. Its venom can be deadly to dogs, so care must be taken in places such as the Lake District and the Hampshire New Forest. One of the creators of the Patterdale terrier, Frank Buck, had a terrier with this name and which was a famous worker.

Alston
Archie
Adler
Aubrey
Aniseed
Adele
Avens
Alto
Alice
Arrow
Angelica
Aster
Alison
Alum
Allegro
Astie
Allie
Acky
Autumn
Auburn
Alder
Ash
Asher
Ashton
Alice
Addy
Abby
Atlas
Avril
Ava
Alf

Alfie: Neil Wilson's terrier, bred by the author and featuring on the cover of The Lakeland Terrier. Alfie was a grand worker and saw much action at mink. He had the typical slape coat of Breay/Buck bred Patterdales, from which he was descended.
Alfred
Archer
Arnie
Arnold
Absynth
Anvil

B:

Brash: rootstock and low shrubbery in stripped forestry.
Bash
Basher
Barney
Bart; from *The Simpsons* fame.
Brunswick
Blenim
Becker
Beckett
Bellows
Blethyn
Blythe
Brett
Brian
Basil
Beech
Beechy
Baton
Breton
Burdoch
Bulrush
Bluebell
Broom
Brush; Cyril Breay's last terrier.
Bryony
Bugle

Beagler
Bugler
Buckle
Briton
Baltimore
Bracket
Brigg
Blagg
Bragg
Bodie; James Herriot (real name Alf Wight) had a border terrier with this name.
Blackett; the name of the children in Arthur Ransome's *Swallows and Amazons*.
Blen; shortened form of Blencathra, a Lakeland mountain where Sharp Edge has claimed a number of lives over the years.
Ben
Benny
Betty; once a popular name for Lakeland terriers bred and owned by folk local to the Lake District in particular. Braithwaite Wilson's Betty was a truly excellent worker at the Ullswater Foxhounds and one of the foundation bitches of Sid Wilkinson's famous strain of Lakeland terrier.
Barley
Boozer: the name of the grandsire of my dog Ghyll who was another great worker.
Britt: Maurice Bell's famous black terrier which was lethal with foxes.
Bruce
Briar; another English name for a blackberry bush.
Bow
Bess
Brow
Bowson
Blackberry
Bilberry
Blueberry
Berry
Borran; a naturally formed rockpile in the Lakes.

Bruin
Brunt
Brant; meaning 'steep' in old Lake District fell parlance and a term that is still used by some today. Brant was one of Willie Irving's first terriers and the cornerstone of his strain.
Brittle
Bramble; yet another term for a blackberry bush.
Brock; an old country term for a badger, as in 'Bill Brock.'
Breeze
Bonnie
Bone
Biddie
Beano: Oliver Gill's well known typey dog terrier which was bred down from Breay/Buck stock.
Bantam
Banter
Basher
Bashful
Butcher: One of the two terriers trapped near Brotherswater for several days in 1948. Butcher was rescued.
Badger: The other terrier which died as a result of being trapped in 1948.
Bink
Bodger: Stan Mattinson's famous terrier which saw service at the Coniston Foxhounds and which greatly impressed Anthony Chapman.
Blacky
Blacksmith; a famous Patterdale terrier had this name.
Boss: One of Irving's Lakeland terriers which saw service at the Melbreak Foxhounds during the same era as his famous Turk.
Buster
Brick
Bricky
Bleak
Blue
Buzz
Bracken; my own dog is called Bracken and he is a real character and big personality, as well as a great bushing dog, being a basset

hound cross.

Billy; another country term for a badger and a name frequently used for terriers in particular. Sanderson's Billy was likely one of the ancestors of the Breay/Buck strain.

Bobby; I knew a Jack Russell terrier with this name. He was the leader of a pack running loose on a local farm near where I grew up and he was an eager ratter, shifting some big rats as they moved between food supplies and a warm bed in the barn.

Bedlam; a suitable name for a noisy dog.

Bella: I had a bitch terrier with this name. Most of her litter mates were of typical Breay/Buck type, but she threw back to the old Bedlington and was a large, scruffy terrier with a poor coat.

Bingo: Breay's famous fox killing dog terrier.

Blitz: Breay's terrier bred during the Second World War.

Barker; an ancestor of the modern Patterdale terrier had this name.

Beck; a Lakeland stream, or brook and my current bitch terrier, though she is now too old for work.

Breck; from the hero of the novel *Kidnapped*, Alan Breck.

Buffer

Brim

Bitters

Brook; a northern name for a stream.

Barrister

Barrack

Betsy

Becky

Belcher; this name would have suited one of my own dogs, which belched very loudly after every meal. I must have laughed every day of the ten or more years I had him, before he had to be put to sleep due to the ravages of old age, but only after leaving my wife and I with some great memories.

Brockley

Brinkley; the name of the dog featured in the classic film *You've Got Mail* – one of my all-time favourites.

Bellman

Bowman

Bruntley

Brandle

Baldrick; of *Black Adder* fame.
Bradley
Butch; another of our dogs. Butch was as tough as 'owd boots, having survived distemper when he was a puppy. This disease had a massive mortality rate during the 1970s, but Butch pulled through after a few weeks of seriously ill health. He died at the age of thirteen, after going to sleep under a bush and never waking up – a peaceful end to a hectic life.
Bertha; a hill not far from where I grew up is known as Big Bertha. It is a lovely wild spot and is glorious in August, when the heather is in full purple bloom, when a fox or two has been flushed from this spot.
Buster;
Bobbin; used for cotton. The bobbin-turning industry once flourished in and around the English Lake District and Tommy Dobson learned this trade.

C:

Cherry
Charlie; an old English name for a fox, or one of the hero's of the wonderful *Darling Buds of May*.
Chance
Chancel
Cyril
Clement
County
Celery
Campion
Charlock
Chicory
Chervil
Clarry
Clover
Comfret
Comfrey
Cockle
Cockler
Corn

Carrock
Cob
Cowslip
Cranberry
Chez
Chaz
Chancer
Chain
Cleeve; a regional name for a steep valley in Devon, such as those found on Dartmoor and Exmoor. This can also be rendered 'Cleave.'
Crag; a feature of mountainous landscape such as that found in Cumbria, Derbyshire and North Wales.
Crags; I knew a black bitch with this name and a cracking worker. She was lost in a deep rock earth at an old quarry while working fox.
Crevice; This dog often worked alongside Crags and was another cracking worker from the Breay/Buck strain. In fact, Crags and Crevice may well have been bred by Frank Buck during the early 1980s.
Chain; as in the 'Pennine Chain.'
Cora
Cobbler
Cal
Carron; a place in County Clare, Ireland.
Cackle
Cackler
Carlton
Candle
Chandler; of *Friends* fame.
Channel
Clonmel; a Southern-Irish town.
Chorister
Choral
Chorus
Clegg
Cleggy; a main character in the classic *Last of the Summer Wine*.
Cassy; this black bitch was very typey and the grand-dam of my

own bitch, Mist.
Candy
Candour
Canter
Caffrey; great Irish ale!
Crab; a popular name for terriers in the Lake District, particularly around Windermere, Grasmere and Coniston. Anthony Chapman's Crab may well have been the Coniston Hunt terrier used to establish his strain during the early 1920s.
Clem
Clemmy
Clam
Clammy
Crofter; a Scottish farmer, or smallholder.
Croft; a Scottish farm or smallholding.
Champ
Caddy
Champer
Cliff
Cryer
Claife; as in Claife Heights on the edge of Windermere.
Chomper
Chomp
Corrie; a regional name for rockpiles under crags in the Scottish Highlands, where foxes, badgers and otters sometimes dwell.
Cairn; a natural rockpile in Scotland, known as a borran in Lakeland. A cairn is also what walkers pile up on the tops of mountains and hills, though the name originally applies to the naturally formed rockpiles of Scotland.
Crest; as in the crest of a hill. Braithwaite Wilson's Crest was bred out of Bowman's Fury and Anthony Chapman's Crab.
Compo; another main character in *Last of the Summer Wine*.
Coin
Cleaver
Connie
Crete; a Breay/Buck bred terrier born during the Second World War.
Clancy

Cartmel; the village and fell in the south Lakeland area.
Cragsman
Craggy
Cashel; the Irish town and castle.
Crafty
Crush
Captain
Capstan
Cosh
Cosher
Con
Carry
Carter
Cromwell
Crescent
Camden
Cass
Chad
Chatter
Chatty
Chess
Cheseden; a famous industrial valley in Lancashire popular with walkers.

D:

Davy; one of the ancestors of the modern Patterdale terrier, which was a great show winner during the 1960s.
Dark
Debby
Dove
Den
Denny
Derby
Dibble
Dibbler
Dribbler
Drizzle
Daffodil

Daisy
Dandelion
Dewsbury
Dewberry
Dock
Dill
Dilly
Diamond
Darky
Dak
Dandy
Dusty
Duster
Derwent; after the river and water in the northern Lake District.
Dobbin; a terrier of this name was the ancestor of Johnny Richardson's strain at the Blencathra Hunt. Breay had great respect for this strain and some Blencathra blood, I suspect, made its way into Breay's strain through Richardson's Tarzan – a dog Breay was most impressed with.
Dodd
Doddick: a farm at the foot of Blencathra Fell.
Doug
Daker
Deadlock; the famous hound in the novel, *Tarka the Otter*.
Dusk
Dusky
Dent; a charming North Yorkshire village huddled between the wild fells. A Breay bred terrier, Monty, belonging to John Nicholson at the Lunesdale Foxhounds, was lost in a rock hole above Dent Village.
Daz
Dazzle
Dazzler
Dart
Dartmoor
Driver; yet another place-name in areas such as Dartmoor and Exmoor.
Dot

Dottie
Dobbie; another popular name for terriers in the Lake District. Tommy Dobson bred some of the ancestors of modern Lakeland terriers and one of his favourites was called Dobbie.
Dick
Devon
Dell; a remote valley.
Dingle; yet another name for a remote valley, or narrow gorge.
Drayton
Dray
Drayman
Dragman

E:

Eric
Eskdale; A valley in the west Lakes, which is an area of outstanding natural beauty.
Esk
Ellie
Elsa; the lioness in *Born Free*.
Exmoor
Eire; beautiful Ireland.
Etta
Elkie
Elkanah
Emma
Emily
Eyre; as in *Jane Eyre*.
Effie
Edge; the genius guitarist from U2.
Eddie; one of Barry Todhunter's terriers, named after Eddie Chapman.
Ebby
Elsie
Etty
Elderberry
Elder
Elderflower

Elodia
Elymus
Erica
Ernie

F:

Fennel
Flax
Flaxon
Fig
Figoro
Fleming
Farmer
Fury; another popular terrier name in the Lakes in particular and a bitch which was probably one of the ancestors of Breay's strain.
Fern; another name for bracken.
Forester
Fisher
Fen; lowland landscape in places such as Norfolk.
Fly
Fell; Lakeland name for a mountain.
Fricker
Flicker
Fangs
Fipps
Fritter
Fran
Franny
Fox
Foxy
Ferodo
Floss
Frisk; taken from a Cumbrian hunting song.
Foiler; a popular name for fox terriers during the late nineteenth century.
Frolic
Fan
Fuss

Fanny
Fussy
Fleet
Fleetwith; a mountain in the heart of the Lakes, where Honister Quarry is situated.
Fog
Foggy; one of the main characters in the classic *Last of the Summer Wine*.
Fred
Freddy
Flick
Foss; a name for a waterfall and pool in North Yorkshire, where shepherds used to dip their flocks of sheep.
Flock
Frock
Forest
Frederick
Foil
Foiler
Fitz
Fry
Fryor
Freeze
Fathom
Farthing
Folly
Frith
Firkin
Flip
Flipper
Flapper
Flap
Flag
Flagon
Frankie
Fritter
Fricker

G:
Gin
Garlic
Goose
Griff
Griffon
Gentian
Ginny
Glitz
Grouse
Gromit; from *Wallace and Gromit*.
Grade
Grader
Gitters
Ginger
Gem; a famous ancestor of the Patterdale terrier of today.
Grip; a popular name for terriers.
Griff
Growl
Growler
Gruff
Geoff
Gen
Granite; a very hard rock.
Glen; a valley.
Glenny
Gillert; legend has it that a dog of this name killed the last wolf in Britain.
Gypsy
Galley
Gallion
Gallon
Gallery
Ghyll; a steep ravine in Lakeland.
Gill
Gillie; a river keeper in Scotland.
Gyp; a popular name for terriers in the Lakes up until about the

1940s, after which it fell out of fashion.
Gravel
Gordon
Gaffer
Gravy
Gradient
Gradely
Gad
Gadder
Gladsome
Glad
Gladys
Gercher; a London slang name.
Gotcha
Greta; a river that runs through Keswick in Cumbria.
Gator
Grenville; a character in the classic *Open All Hours*.
Glitters
Grapple
Grappler
Gossan
Gosling

H:

Hatty
Hawthorn
Hollyhock
Hysopp
Horseradish
Hassle
Hassler
Hawk
Hawker
Heath
Hemlock
Honeysuckle
Hetty
Hooch; from the film *Turner and Hooch*.

Hook
Hock
Hops
Hoppy
Hopple
Hoppler
Hockle
Hockler
Hocks
Hooker
Heckler
Hobby
Hobbler
Hobble
Hunter
Huntsman
Henry; I once knew a boxer with this name and he was a huge, muscular dog. The family was never burgled while he was in the house!
Heather; as in a heather-moor.
Heath
Heathcliffe
Henchman
Hacksaw
Hacker
Hem
Honey
Hornet
Hazel
Hyacinth; as in Mrs Bucket from *Keeping Up Appearances*.
Hackle
Hackler
Harriet
Hemmy
Harry
Helvellyn; a Lakeland mountain that has claimed many lives over the years, where the infamous Striding Edge is located.
Hedger

Hedge
Holker
Hark
Harker; Tom Harker, the poacher from the wonderfully evocative *The Shooting Party*.
Harmony
Harmonica
Hassle
Hassler
Hemp
Heckle
Heckler
Hessler

I:
Ice
Iris
Iggy
Ivy
Icey
Ike; yet another Lake District terrier name, as in Red Ike, the famous terrier bred by Albert Benson in 1932 and which served at the Blencathra Foxhounds and Coniston Foxhounds, becoming a legendary worker which ran loose with hounds. Ike was living proof that big terriers could still be useful, even in deep borrans. He was the ancestor of Breay and Buck's terriers bred after the 1930s.
Itsy
Imogen
Inca
Ickle
Inkling
Idyll
Isher
Ishla
Ismay
Islay
Isla

J:
Jasper
Jill
Jitters
Jingles
Jiggles
Juggler
Jeeves; of *Jeeves and Wooster* fame.
Jilly
Jake
Jasper
Juddy
Jelly
Jakey
Jen
Jenny
Jet
Jed
Jude
Judy
Jess
Jessy
Jello
Joe
Jack
Jacky
Jummy
Jimmy; bred out of Breay/Buck stock and used by Roger Westmorland at the Coniston Foxhounds where he proved most useful.
Jumbo; an old fashioned name once popular for early fell and Lakeland terriers. Jumbo was a famous Coniston terrier of the early part of the twentieth century which successfully shifted foxes from the incredibly deep and dangerous Broad How Borran situated on the fells above the Kirkstone Pass.
Jock
Jockey

Jim
Jig
Jiggy
Jiggle
Jaggers; the lawyer in Charles Dickens wonderful tale *Great Expectations*.
Jud
Juddy
Jester
Jest
Jelly
Jel
Jemma
Jem
Jemmy
Jerky
Jangles
Jerrod
Jarrod
Jarrock
Jonty
Jaunt
Jaunter
Jorrocks; the character from Surtees novels and a terrier bred by Willie Irving during the late 1940s. Jorrocks was an outstandingly good looking Lakeland terrier, the best type Irving ever produced according to the man himself, who was also a good worker.

K:
Kate
Katrine
Kim
Kit
Kitty
Kimmy
Kimbel
Kibbles: a mining term.
Kip

Kipps
Kipper; a brother of Breay's Rusty and ancestor of Brian Nuttall's strain of Patterdale terrier which have greatly influenced modern breeding.
Kerry; a county in Ireland of outstanding natural beauty.
Keeper; the name of Emily Bronte's dog, which featured in Charlotte Bronte's novel *Shirley*.
Kelly; a Coniston terrier of the 1920s walked at Troutbeck Park and a grand worker.
Kettle
Kettley
Kettler
Kendal; a Cumbrian town considered as the gateway to the Lakes.
Ken
Kenny
Kentish
Kemp
Karry
Kes; from the book and film.

L:

Lucy
Lucius
Luscious
Lace
Lacey
Lavender
Lindon
Linton
Liquorice
Lyle
Lucius
Lucas
Lett
Letty
Lentle
Line
Lil

Lilly
Liner
Lyne
Lindy
Lad
Laddie
Loppy
Ling; another name for moorland heather.
Lintle
Lendle
Liddle
Link
Lank
Lanky
Lumber; a great name for a mischievous puppy.
Lambert
Lumpton
Lana
Laura
Lara
Lister
Lawyer
Linker
Link
Lester
Lemon
Lilt
Lilter

M:

Monty
Mellow
Marigold
Marjoram
Mistletoe
Mustard
Malva
Marram

May
Meadow
Molina
Mercury
Mars
Mellick
Melling
Mantle
Mizzen
Mast
Master
Matey
Massey
Morris
Mick; another well known terrier from Breay and Buck's breeding programme.
Mickey
Mess
Messy
Moss; a popular name for sheepdogs.
Mossy
Myrt
Myrtle; popular in Cumbria for terriers.
Mischief
Meg
Megan
Mol
Molly
Moley; Cyril Breay's brother-in-law, Machin, had a famous terrier by this name. Machin lived in Lincolnshire and had some great terriers, being a keen badger digger and hunter of foxes. Breay married Machin's sister after divorcing his first wife. Breay dug a litter of cubs at Garsdale with Jossie Akerigg and gave them to Machin to rear, who may have sold them to the local hunt for restocking the country after distemper or mange had decimated the population. Breay spent time in Lincolnshire digging with Machin.
Malone
Mock

Mocky
Murphy; a good Irish name.
Mint
Minty
Minter
Mist; I had a terrier by this name and she was a real character. After giving birth to her new litter of puppies I got her all settled in and was off to bed, when she kicked-up the most tremendous fuss, as though telling me not to leave her alone "with this lot!" I had to sleep on the sofa and keep her company that night, though afterwards she was fine. She was mostly bred along Patterdale terrier lines.
Misty
Miller
Mister
Muster
Maple
Maggie
Mags
Mandy
Miner; a good name for a terrier, which were originally bred to go down holes in the ground. One of Brian Nuttall's best workers was known by this name.
Mona
Mel
Melly
Melbreak; a fell above Crummock Water in the Lakes.
Magda
Midge
Midget
Mac
Mike
Major
Marshal
Milly
Marsh
Mallow
Mickle

Mickeline
Mite
Matey
Mangle
N:
Nancy
Nip
Nipper
Nippy
Nightingale
Nightshade
Nickel
Nidge
Nigel
Nell
Nellie
Newsboy
Narvik
Ness
Nessy; affectionate nickname for the mysterious Loch Ness Monster.
Nessa
Nettle
Nelson
Nectar
Nicely
Nan
Nance
Nanny
Narnia
Nando
O:
Ossler
Oscar
Onion
Oregamo

Ottis
Oat
Orchid
Orchard
Orca; of killer whale fame.
Otter
Oxen
Ox
Oz; from the famous film.
Ozzy
Oak
Oaken
Oakley
Otto
Ode
Oddjob
Ockle
Okra

P:

Polly
Pinky
Primrose
Perk
Perks; a character out of the wonderful tale *The Railway Children*.
Polar
Perky
Printer
Parsley
Parsnip
Pansy
Pearl
Peppermint
Peter
Pike; a name associated with Lakeland mountains, as well as a fish popular with anglers.
Piker
Pennine; a mountain chain in England running from Derbyshire into

the borders of England and Scotland, and very popular with walkers.
Pen
Penny
Prunella
Pilot
Paddy
Perry
Pestle
Purple
Pitch
Pitcher
Pat
Patty
Poker
Pobble
Pedal
Pedlar
Peeler; another name for a policeman in Ireland.
Preston
Piper; a common name for terriers in the north-east of England.
Percy
Pep
Pepper
Pauper
Pamper
Phoenix
Pitcher
Peppy
Pip; the hero of the novel *Great Expectations*.
Pet
Petty
Port
Porter
Punch
Pickle
Patch
Prickle

Pig
Piggy
Pont
Panda
Promise
Porthole
Q:
Quill
Quiller
Queen
Queenie
Quantum
Quartz
Quell
Queller
Quarry
Quarryman
R:
Roger
Rice
Raspberry
Rhubarb
Rose
Rosey
Rosemary
Ralph
Rye
Rudyard
Rush
Royal
Renegade
Renny
Rennard
Renold
Rigg; place-name and a name for fells in the Lakes.
Ranter

Ransom
Russland
Russ
Rags
Race
Racer
Riff
Ruff
Ruffler
Rift
Riss
Rick
Ricky
Rock
Rocky
Red
Reel
Reeler
Rebel
Rex
Rydal; a small place in Cumbria between Ambleside and Grasmere.
Rusty
Rocket
Rattle
Rattler
Ruthless
Ruth
Roy
Rastus
Rufford; a place near Sherwood Forest.
Robin
Ross
Rally
Ridge
Reef
Reeder
Reed
Ranger

Romper; a good name for the lively sort!
Runswick
Rook
Raven

S:

Steel
Spout
Stout
Steeler
Schooner
Swallow; the boat of *Swallows and Amazons*.
Spout
Spark
Sparky
Skiffle; Cyril Breay's very typey bitch which was also a wonderful worker.
Sid
Sidney
Stamp
Stamper
Shade
Shadow
Selwyn
Stan
Stanley
Snap
Snapper
Snappy
Snatch
Sally
Sal
Scandal
Spiff
Spiffy
Stream
Snip
Sett

Settle
Settler
Sherry
Shaft
Stoper
Steamer
Straddle
Saddle
Saddler
Shady
Scamp
Shandy
Socks
Sam
Sammy
Samuel
Storm
Stormer
Smithy; shortened title for a blacksmith.
Smitty
Squeak
Squeaky
Squeaker
Stump
Stumpy
Sheena
Spider
Sassy
Silver
Silk
Silky
Selkie
Skip
Skipper
Skippy; of *Skippy the Kangaroo* fame.
Skittle
Skittles
Skittler

Sedge
Smudge
Smudger
Sting
Stinger
Sharp
Sharper
Sharpy
Sharky
Scree; loose rock found on the fellsides in the Lake District.
Slate
Selwyn
Spiffy
Shandy
Sheena
Saffron
Sage
Shallot
Sorrel
Shepherd
Strawberry
Samphire
Star
Snowdrop
Silas
Slater
Slatt
Shake
Shaker
Skaky
Slattery
Sheik
Shallow
Sherman
Sheila
Shiraz
Seeker
Scramble

Scrambler
Shack
Shaft
Settler
Settle; a charming market town in North Yorkshire.
T:
Tosh
Tar
Tarsus
Trammer
Toiler
Toil
Tailer
Trail
Trailer
Tarry
Tim
Tarragon
Thistle
Thyme
Traveller
Tway
Tay
Tween
Timothy
Thwaite
Trim
Trimmer
Timmy
Tess
Tessy
Tessa
Tessle
Tressle
Tipple
Tippler
Tuppence

Thruppence
Trent; a river that flows through Nottinghamshire.
Trencher
Trench
Tweel
Twyne
Tweed; a famous salmon fishing river in Scotland.
Tweedy
Titch
Titchy
Techy
Tickle
Tickler; another terrier given to Buck by Breay during the 1930s.
Tarn; a small body of water usually found out on the fells of the Lake District.
Tat
Tats
Tatters
Tatty
Teddy
Ted
Trace
Tracer
Topple
Toppler
Tink
Tinker
Tinky
Tinkle
Tyson
Tan
Tanner
Tandy
Tandem
Tear 'Em; a famous name for terriers in the fells of Cumbria and one of the ancestors of modern Patterdale terriers which was bred by Jim Fleming out of Myrt.
Twist

Twister
Tiger; the famous bitch Breay gave to Buck after the Bishopdale rescue.
Tigress
Tigger
Tiggle
Tig; another of Breay's terriers which was an excellent worker.
Tiggy
Tarzan; a terrier bred by Johnny Richardson of the Blencathra Foxhounds and one greatly admired by Breay. I suspect that at some point during the late 1940s or into the 1950s Breay used Tarzan or a son of Tarzan as outcross blood.
Trouble
Troubles
Teeze
Teezer
Teezy
Tizzy
Tip
Trader
Tex
Texas
Texan
Taffy
Tangy
Tango
Taff
Trilby
Terry; one of the foundation terriers of the Oregill strain of Lakeland terrier and one which served at the Melbreak Foxhounds.
Turban
Topsy
Topol
Toppy
Toppler
Topple
Turk; an old Scottish farming term and a Scottish place-name, as in Brig O' Turk.

Tarquin
Tarka; as in *Tarka the Otter*, a famous novel and film.
Tom
Thomas
Tommy
Tomlin
Trix
Trixie
Tina
Tony
Tartar
Tyrant
Trick
Tricky
Trickster
Trap
Trappy
Trinket
Tack
Tackle
Tackler
Twile
Thorn
Thornton
Thornham
Thornly
Task
Tasker
Tasky
Tyne; a famous north-east river.
Tynedale
Tab
Tabby
Tubb
Tubby; a terrier bred out of the Coniston red dog and Wendy.
Trade
Trader

U:
Ulpha; a place in Lakeland.
Ulster
Ultra
Uz
Uzzar
Uckle
Uist

V:
Vandal
Venus
Vim
Vimmy
Vixen
Venture
Viper; another name for an adder and one of Buck's terriers had this name.
Vicky
Vic
Venom
Vent
Vee
Vye
Vermont
Vender
Vimto
Vintner
Vinnie
Violet
Vernon
Veronica
Vetch
Viola
Vine

W:
Whip

Wallace; of *Wallace and Gromit* fame.
Whippy
Whin
Whinny
Wren
Woodruff
Woody; as in *Woody Woodpecker*.
Woodman
Warren
Wilmot
William
Worry
Willow
Winnow
Wist
Wisty
Wister
Welcome
Wasp; another common name for fell and Lakeland terriers.
Wendy; the foundation bitch of modern Patterdale terriers. She saw much work in the Mallerstang district and every fox she bolted in this area was accounted for by Breay using a twelve-bore shotgun.
Whisky; another terrier belonging to Machin which was a great finder.
Whisk; a son of Turk of Melbreak and a famous fox killer of the 1930s.
Whiskers; an important brood bitch in Breay's strain.
Will
Whitby
Witty
Whittle
Whittler
Whittles
Willie
Whistle
Whistler
Wanton
Worton

Winkle
Winkler
Welton
Wilton
Wilt
Walt

X:

Xanadu
Xavier
Xerxes

Y:

York
Yorkshire
Yorky
Yoeman; a gentleman farmer.
Yarrow; a yellow wild flower.
Yetty
Yellow
Yell
Yak
Yaz
Yasmin
Yum
Yummy

Z:

Zena
Zealot
Zebra
Zumba
Zidan
Zeb
Zebby
Zak
Zad
Zadie
Zakry

Zinca
Zinky
Zinc
Zondra
Zilcher
Zilch

Other Books by Sean Frain include;
The Border-Lakeland Terrier
Last Lair of Wolves (2nd edition) – An Inspector Le Fleming Mystery – *"A must read. Kept me gripped. Brilliantly written."* – H. Harrison, Artist. *"The best book I've read lately."* – Carol Breakey on Facebook.
Murder, Mystery & Mischief in the English Lake District – *"It's so addictive."* – Jane Hart.
All available on Amazon Books & Kindle ebooks.

"Sean Frain & Wainwright – put them both in your backpack." – Alrene Hughes – Author

Last Lair of Wolves

An Inspector Le Fleming Mystery

Sean Frain

This book received rave reviews in 2015

Printed in Great Britain
by Amazon